KNOCKED SIDEWAYS

Discover the extraordinary power of hope

Always have hope! ♡

Sarah McGeough

Knocked Sideways

First edition independently published by Sarah McGeough in the United Kingdom 2024.

A CIP catalogue record of this book is available from the British Library

ISBN 978-1-8382767-5-1 (hardcover)
ISBN: 978-1-8382767-7-5 (paperback)
Cover design: Jenn Garside
Editor: Christine Beech
Typesetting: Matthew J Bird

For further information about this book, please contact the author at:
sarah@writenowcoaching.co.uk

To Edward. The sunshine in my life.

Love always, Mumma x

Contents

Foreword

'It's not how you got in the crocodile's mouth. It's how you get out.'

Sage advice my grandmother would share, pretty much every time I complained about something going wrong. And she was right.

Especially as these were not life-altering events. Mine were, what now appear to be, trivial moments. Falling out with a friend, messing up my homework or upsetting a parent. They were not life or death, but that mantra stayed with me.

You are about to read over twenty great escapes from crocodile mouths of every shape and size. Some will make you gasp, many will make you cry and all have common themes that run, unstoppable, through these pages like rivers to the sea.

The human spirit is remarkable. When faced with life's greatest challenges a hidden switch is flicked, a spark ignites and the opportunity to rise is presented. Not everyone climbs. Some weaken, blame others, cry 'poor me' and languish in the crocodile's jaws. Others rise, escape limitations and go on to be bolder, better, incredible people. They use their experiences as fuel, they turn rocks into stepping stones and, most importantly, they inspire others.

Between the gasps and the tears, I promise you will be inspired as you read this book. You will be questioned and advised by the author. You will be stirred to take action, to appreciate your own life and you will give thanks as you realise just how fortunate you are.

Take this inspiration and turn it into action. Use one thing from every story and apply it in your life. No one plans to be *Knocked Sideways* but, when you are, and you will be, remember the motivation from these pages and move on, move out, move up.

Michael Heppell
Author, Speaker, Coach

An Idea

The idea for this book came when I finally landed back on my feet. In the space of five years, I had dealt with emergency surgery to save my life, my mum having a nervous breakdown and nearly dying, realising IVF was not going to be the answer to having a family, being made redundant from a career I loved, not coping with the transition of becoming a parent and just about hanging onto my marriage.

All those layers of complex emotions had sent me on a downward spiral. I was feeling bruised and bashed and grasping onto the fact that I was enjoying learning new skills as a coach. But, I knew deep inside that I had lost my way and could not see where my life was heading.

I needed help, but I was not sure where to find it.

When the global pandemic hit in 2020, we had only just relocated from North London to East Sussex to start our 'new life'. Our excitement turned to panic and we had no clue how we were going to cope. But, when I look back, I realise that pause gave me exactly what I needed. As our pace of life slowed down, I was able to reflect and spend valuable time with my boys. It was the perfect opportunity to balance myself, reignite my passions and find ME again.

After a walk along the beach with my best friend, in our permitted hour of exercise, new ideas started to form and I came away with the incredible thought that maybe I could write a book.

Six months later, I became a published author, which lit a very significant light. It made me see life through a different lens. I discovered a creative flare hidden inside me, connected with a brilliant online community and felt a tingle of excitement for the future.

But where does my fighting spirit and tenacity come from?

What makes a person determined to get back up?

I knew there was another book idea niggling inside me. So, I decided to ask others.

This is… *Knocked Sideways.*

Be Inspired

'Life is about change. Sometimes it's painful, sometimes it's beautiful, but most of the time it's both'
– Kristen Kreuk

Being *knocked sideways* can mean different things. It can be a knock-you-off-balance moment that changes your life, or smaller blips that rattle you for a while which may then stack up to become much bigger. Needless to say, they can all lead to similar feelings... A sense of doom deep inside. An impact that brings a maelstrom of emotions and confusion that can cause a mental shake-up. You cannot focus and are struggling day to day. Your head is spinning. You feel lacklustre. You feel broken. You are floating with no grasp on reality. You are not sure if you will ever feel the same again.

In essence, it feels like a dark cloud that will not shift.

The reality is that life is never a straight line. You will have to navigate difficult situations and the lessons you learn will be hard, but you must not lose sight of who you are when you feel at rock bottom. It can be scary to feel trapped in never-ending pain, grief, anger, anxiety and endless waves of stress, but it is important that you choose not to remain stuck there.

Why do some people allow challenging times and troubled thoughts to halt their lives and become all-consumed, while others find a way out and are able to reignite their lives? As humans, it has been suggested that we are born with a negative bias. This way of thinking can take us down a dark path, if we let it take control. The truth is we have our own way of dealing with things. Two people may lose the same person or be involved in the same accident, but how they react may be remarkably different.

You have to find your own recovery position.

A place where you are balanced, safe and happy.

How do you feel about your life right now? Honestly?

You are about to feel inspired to live your life.

Inside are 21 life-changing stories from amazing men and women with a variety of personal *knocked sideways* moments that left them reeling in a pathway of heartache and uncertainty. What they have in common is that they all chose to have the courage to move forward. They wanted to share their stories so that you can be encouraged to do the same.

Each chapter offers my reflections which highlight brilliant tools and techniques so you can build resilience, boost your confidence, create a healthier mindset and ultimately love your life.

You cannot change what has happened, but you can change what happens next.

1

Joshua Robertson

'Where there's a will there's a way' – Albert Einstein

The last thing I remember was shouting, "Go faster, it will be bumpier."

Four months later, I woke up in hospital.

When I was 10, my parents separated. My mum decided that she wanted to move back to Adelaide, Australia, and asked if I wanted to join her. I jumped at the chance. I started at the local school soon after our move and quickly made new friends. I joined the Marion Swimming Club and was thrilled when I won third place and received a medal. I was sure I would be a professional swimmer or sportsman one day. I had it all planned out in my head.

At 11, my whole life changed. My parents let me go away with some friends for the Christmas holidays to stay on a farm in Victoria. We enjoyed the freedom and loved chasing kangaroos and koalas. On Christmas Eve, one of my friends suggested that we take a quad bike for a spin around the farm. Neither of us had helmets and there were no adults around to notice. I remember whizzing across the land and having fun. But then everything went dark.

I woke up in a hospital bed with brain damage and a physical disability.

I remember thinking, "What's going on? Why am I in hospital?" My parents were by my bedside. I wanted to ask them but was unable to speak. They explained that the quad bike had smashed into a fence post, with me on it. My friend had jumped off, at the last moment, but was knocked unconscious. He woke up two hours later and alerted his parents, who called for help. An air ambulance arrived and pronounced me dead. Miraculously, they used CPR to revive me. I was in a bad way; my head was smashed in and my body was a mess. The handlebar of the quad bike had punctured my spleen and barbed wire was embedded in my face.

They told me everything I had missed over the last four months. I had been flown to the Royal Children's Hospital in Melbourne where I was placed in a coma for three months. I was then transferred to the Women's and Children's Hospital in Adelaide, where I was unconscious for a month. My head had swollen to double its size and the doctors told my family those awful words, 'to expect the worst'. They said I was unlikely to survive and, if I did, I would not be able to walk or talk. A specialist doctor performed surgery to drain the fluid from my brain and rebuild my skull using metal plates. He was not sure of the outcome. It was a life-or-death procedure but, against all the odds, it was a success.

Then started my long road to recovery.

Learning to live life with a disability was challenging. I had to learn how to walk and talk again. I lost my sense of balance and the brain damage caused spasticity in my hands. I had to find new ways to use and move my body. The support and encouragement from my family was the reason I made such amazing progress. My mum helped me to walk again by doing daily physio exercises. My brother, who was a teacher in Indonesia, taught me how to speak again. He would show me the word sounds and where to put my tongue to make the different noises; almost like how you would teach a baby to talk. When my dad visited from the UK, he would practise hand exercises with me. He was a tai chi instructor, so he knew all the right muscles to target in the early stages. It was tough adapting to the way my body was moving.

There were emotional challenges too. Everyone I knew, before the accident, treated me differently. I remember when I was 14 years old, life felt difficult and was getting too much for me. One day, I wanted to watch *The Simpsons* and my sister would not turn the TV over. It sounds crazy, I know, but usually I would have fought with her to get the remote, but I could not and that upset me. The reality of my disability hit home, so I asked my little sister to grab a kitchen knife and stab me in the heart. It was a shocking thing to say, but I felt helpless.

When I was about 15, I watched my friends enjoying themselves having a play fight and said to one of them, "Punch me as hard as you can." They would not do it. That hurt more than a punch ever would. I wanted my friends to treat me the same. Going from being able-bodied to living with a physical disability is not easy to come to terms with. I struggled with mental health through my teens, until I learned how to focus my energy on something positive.

I discovered my secret weapon. Humour.

When I left school, I had no idea what I was going to do. All my friends had dreams of the careers they wanted and knew the direction their lives were heading. I felt stuck. What could I do? I felt useless. One day, my friend said to me, "Josh, you're pretty funny, why don't you try stand-up comedy? There's an open mic night in town at The Rhino Room."

As soon as I stepped on stage, I knew it was where I was destined to be. I have never looked back. It felt amazing to hear an entire room erupt into laughter because of me. It meant so much that they were not laughing at me; they were laughing with me. Stand-up comedy helped me deal with my disability. Making people laugh allowed me the opportunity to get away from my issues and problems. You could say it provided respite from my disability.

As my confidence as a comedian grew, I started to branch out by doing shows in Adelaide, Sydney and Melbourne. I wanted more and was itching to find opportunities on the comedy scene. London seemed the best place, so I moved back to live with my dad and stepmum. They facilitated most of my comedy career and took me on trips to Berlin, Indonesia, New York, the Edinburgh Fringe Festival and all over the UK to fulfil my passion for comedy.

My love of comedy connected me to a new love.

I was performing at the Backyard Comedy Club in Bethnal Green. I got on stage, as usual, with the help of my carer. He positioned me on stage and left me to it. There was a lady in the front row who was laughing and caught my attention. Sitting next to her was the woman who would end up being my fiancée. At the end of the show, I asked her to connect with me on Facebook, which was the start of a wonderful relationship.

A few years into dating, I received exciting news that I was going to be a dad. I decided this was the right time to propose and wanted to do it on the stage where we first met. I booked myself a gig at the Backyard Comedy Club and invited all our friends and family. My biggest fear was falling over, so I spent weeks practising. During my set, I called out for a volunteer to help with a new joke. I then called for 'the blonde woman at the back.' She came up on stage from a different side to the one I had been practising. I panicked. She ended up having to hold me so that I did not fall over, but I still managed to get down on one knee and propose. I got the reply I was expecting, "Yeah, man" (my catchphrase). The whole room then erupted in claps and whistles and everyone stood up to cheer us on.

My love of comedy, and making people laugh, has connected me to many amazing people and opportunities. One night, I went to an open mic in London and was approached by a choreographer called Thomas Michael Voss. He said he had been watching the way I walked and thought I would be perfect to help him create a dance piece he was working on. We collaborated closely for months to create *Questio* which is a dance interpretation, portraying the pressures that men face to be 'manly'. I danced live on stage in The Place in London Euston, and it was amazing. Comedy always keeps my brain ticking over but performing the dance piece kept my body active. I had to work hard on my balance and coordination. Thomas had been battling cancer while we worked together and he sadly passed away, shortly after the production. In his memory, we took *Questio* on tour in Sweden. After the tour, BBC3 aired a series called *Amazing Humans* and they asked me to share a bit of my story.

Having my first child was nothing short of a miracle. I am a very proud dad and count my blessings that I have been able to have two beautiful children. They keep me on my toes and I love spending as much time with them as I can. Being a disabled father has many challenges, but over the years I have found my own way to make sure they have their needs met and do not miss out on opportunities. It helps that my children are kind, understanding and loving. I know they see me for who I am, as a person, and take my disability in their stride.

The film director, David Abramsky, spotted me in the Top-Secret Comedy Club, in Covent Garden, and was blown away by my performance. He told me, "I haven't been able to get your jokes out of my head. I thought to myself, this guy needs to be on screen." We worked together for a year and, with a lot of hard work, the short film *Dad Joke* became a reality. I was the star of the 16-minute film which premiered at the BFI London Film Festival and was shown at the London Short Film Festival. There are plans to develop a six-part TV series with the help of the Edinburgh Talent Lab Connects scheme.

Living with a disability can take its toll on your mental health and I always make sure I keep that in check. It would be easy for me to sit in a chair all day and give up because it is all too hard. I became an ambassador for the organisation *Calmer* and a champion for the *Be Kind Movement*, which both promote better mental health. Doing charity work gives me a sense of purpose and makes me happy, knowing that I am helping other people. Also, being included and accepted for who I am within the charity gives me a real confidence boost. Being happy and confident allows me to be more productive.

I have achieved one of my long-term goals of performing a 20-minute spot at the London Comedy Store. I rocked the room and, when I finished my set, I received a standing ovation. In 2021, I received an award from Film London called *London Lodestars* and Best Lead Actor for my performance in *Dad Joke* at the Oxford International Short Film Festival. I have big plans for the future. I aim to tour the UK, Australia and America with my comedy show, act in more TV and film, and work on more writing projects for TV. I am excited to perform at the Brighton and Edinburgh Fringe Festivals. Sadly, I am no longer engaged, but my new show *Enable Me* gives me the right platform to express myself and talk about our breakup.

I have always been extremely self-motivated and ambitious. It is all about having a positive 'can do' attitude. Having a disability has taught me a lot and made me a better person. Things can change at the drop of a hat but, just because you have lost what you once had, it does not mean you cannot work with what you now have. I am surrounded by people who love and believe in me and, with them cheering me on, the sky is the limit. I have a physical disability which has made me into the inspirational and determined man I am today. It is part of me.

Becoming disabled was the best mistake I ever made.

Sarah's Reflections

Joshua talked about building confidence through action. You have to start somewhere. Look where you are now, decide where you want to take your life leap… and do it.

Dare to be happy. Joshua did not have anything to smile about after his accident but, with the right support, he was able to deal with his new reality and humour became his medicine. In your darkest times, you can struggle to notice anything that makes you happy, so finding something to laugh about might sound utterly ridiculous. Laughter triggers the release of endorphins, the body's natural feel-good hormone. French surgeon, Henri de Mondeville, always advised telling patients jokes after an operation to relieve pain and aid recovery.

If you force yourself to laugh out loud, it will make a difference. Go on, try it.

Time + hope = happiness. After your lowest moments, there can be hope. It broke my heart to hear Joshua talk about wanting his friends to hit him and his sister to stab him. But just a few years later, he was on stage at the legendary London Comedy Store, making people laugh.

Find your 'thing'. We all have a 'thing' that makes us come alive. For Joshua, it was comedy. He switched his mindset, focused on making people laugh and used his disability to help form his passion, rather than use it as an excuse that would stop him from achieving his goals.

What's your thing?

And how can you make sure you do more of it?

2

Anna Garratt

'Always remember you are braver than you believe, stronger than you seem, smarter than you think and loved more than you know' – Winnie the Pooh

In the summer of 2016, I turned 30. With a demanding job, three young daughters and a busy family, life was chaotic but, with my wonderful husband by my side, we always made it work. I was the fittest and healthiest I had been in years and felt genuinely happy and content.

Shortly after my birthday, I headed away for a girly weekend with friends. I spent a lot of time with one friend who I had met when we were pregnant with our first babies. I knew she had multiple sclerosis (MS), but we had never really spoken about it. She opened up and told me about her experience of diagnosis, the challenges she faced and her unknown future. Like me, she had young children and I remember feeling total admiration for her strength and resilience while thinking how hard it must be raising a family under such uncertainty. I had no idea at the time how significant that conversation would come to be.

A few days later, I noticed a strange numb feeling on the soles of my feet. I was a runner and often had aches and pains, so I shrugged it off. Over the next couple of days, the sensation gradually travelled up my body and I remember sitting at my desk at work and feeling electric shock sensations shooting up my legs. That was the moment the silent panic set in. I have always been a worrier but I tried to be rational and convince myself that it was nothing serious. I listened to my GP telling me that it was probably a virus and my family talking about slipped discs and nerve problems. No one seemed concerned but I had this deep-set anxiety and a voice repeating in my head, "It's MS. It's MS."

The numbness continued to spread and I was admitted to hospital. There was no mention of MS but the doctors were concerned that I might have a life-threatening condition called Guillain-Barré Syndrome. I waited three torturous days in the hospital for an MRI scan. I had too much time to think, I could not sleep and my anxiety grew and grew. By the time I had the scan, my mind was racing and I could not think straight. I am not a religious person but, as I lay inside the machine, I prayed that it was not MS. I prayed that it was not something worse and I prayed for a second chance. A chance to never take my health for granted again.

I sat on my hospital bed for hours, with my husband, waiting for the doctor to come and tell us the results. After what felt like an eternity, he walked over, pulled the curtains and sat on the end of my bed. He had such a kind voice and many words came out of his mouth but all I heard amongst the noise was MS. I never truly understood what people meant when they said their blood ran cold, until that moment. My whole world had just collapsed and I remember rocking back and forth, repeating over and over again, "This isn't happening." It was the first time that I witnessed my wonderful strong husband break down.

In a blur of adrenaline and fear, my family helped me through the next few days. I experienced more symptoms as my whole waist went numb, my hands became stiff and painful electric shock sensations ran down my back whenever I moved.

After more tests and uncertainty, I was discharged, told to remain positive and to live life normally, with a promise that I would be scanned in a few months to see how the disease was progressing. The lows that followed were unbearable and unpredictable. The only way I can describe the feeling is like flipping a switch. I would have days where I felt numb but able to function. Having the girls meant we had to keep things as normal as possible and the daily routine continued. But some days I would wake up and could not face anything. It would come over me like a huge wave and the desperation and fear I felt was indescribable. I was surrounded by love and support, but I had never felt so alone. The same question went around my head constantly, "Why is this happening to me?"

I could not walk past an elderly couple without thinking, "That will never be me and my husband" or see someone in a wheelchair and wonder how long I would have the ability to walk. I would look at my beautiful girls and imagine important milestones I may miss. Or, if I was still there, would I still be 'me'? Would I be able to give them the invaluable support that I was lucky to have from my parents? The difficult thing with MS is that there is no way of knowing how things will pan out. I hear about many people who, 20 or 30 years down the line, are still able-bodied, still working and leading relatively normal lives. But I also hear of people in their 30s and 40s who are wheelchair-bound and need full-time care.

How do you come to terms with the unpredictability of a disease like that?

I still do not know the answer to that question.

I was completely broken. I could not process what was happening to me. But, despite everything, I knew early on that I needed to do whatever it took to bring some positivity out of my situation. I was desperate to blank out my feelings and I thought if I planned and organised something and acted like I was okay, then I might actually start to believe it.

I had friends over one night and while we were sitting chatting and drinking wine they said, "Let's plan something right now. What do you want to do?" Then began our Snowdon challenge. It started with a small group trying to raise a few hundred pounds for charity and turned into an incredible event and was one of the best weekends of my life.

43 of us headed off on that road trip to Wales. It was mid-June, which I had researched to be the month with the least rainfall in Snowdon, but things did not quite go to plan. We were met with torrential rain and 60 mph winds and, on the morning of the climb, we were advised by the rangers not to go ahead. Despite this, we decided we had to give it a go. With an incredible team by my side, we laughed our way through that crazy day. Everyone was soaked before we even left the campsite. We were blown all over that mountain as we trudged up the paths that had quite literally turned into streams. Not for a minute did it dampen our team spirit. I will never forget the laughing, singing, umbrella hats, flasks of whiskey and rainy selfies. We got two-thirds of the way up before we knew it was not safe to continue, but we headed back down with our heads held high. The rain finally stopped, and we took over our flooded campsite, lit the fire pits and had a huge BBQ and an insane amount of cider. That evening was a huge turning point for me. It was the first time that I felt genuinely hopeful. I remember sitting by the fire pit and looking around at all those people I loved, in a flooded field in the middle of rainy Wales, just laughing and having the best time. It was at that moment that I thought, "Maybe it is going to be okay. Maybe I can have MS in my life and still be happy."

As a team, we raised over £10,000 for the MS Trust and, from then on, fundraising became more than a distraction. It became a purpose. I wanted to have positive experiences that I would not have had without my diagnosis. The following year, we organised a charity ball. Once again, what started as a small event snowballed and was a huge success. With the most incredible people by my side, we had an unforgettable evening and raised another £14,000. The following year, on my 33rd birthday, my husband and I did a sponsored skydive. Another experience that I never would have had before my diagnosis. Each event brought a wave of gratitude and positivity which helped to heal me a little more.

It might seem that I am building up to a happily ever after. That I have recovered from the impact of my diagnosis and have an entirely positive mindset about my uncertain future. But life is not that simple. I am a completely different person now. MS coming into my life was the hardest challenge I have ever faced, but it has taught me valuable lessons. In the early days of my diagnosis, I would constantly beat myself up when I felt angry or sad. I would tell myself repeatedly that there were people in far worse situations, and it was not right for me to dwell on it. I know now that I was not being fair to myself.

Looking back, I put an unhealthy amount of pressure on myself to be positive about my situation. I spent a long time trying to figure out how to get through the dark days and whether I was dealing with things in the right way. Trying to figure out where the magic lies. Was it seeing the positives in all situations? Was it jumping out of bed each day and being 100% grateful to be alive? Or was it learning to be realistic about my ability to deal with difficult situations? Knowing there is a process that I was entitled to go through, a process of grief. Honestly, now I think the magic lies in allowing yourself to feel whatever emotions you need to feel, guilt-free. With no time limits, no structure and no rules. To know that you might be fine and at peace with your situation in one minute and, in the next, feel completely devastated. What is vital, is not to let those moments define you as a person. Allow them to happen but get yourself back up and know there is every chance tomorrow will be a better day.

The biggest lesson I have learnt is gratitude. As much as I like to think that I was grateful for my life before MS, in hindsight I do not think I truly was. Health was most definitely something I took for granted. It is hard to explain how differently you see the world after you have experienced something so life-changing. The motivation you gain when, suddenly, your future is unknown and you can no longer assume that your health will remain stable.

My girls have been my biggest motivation from day one. I do not know how I will be in years to come, but I am determined that they will grow up proud of me and know that I did everything I could to make the best of my situation. We have raised them knowing about my condition and we keep things as light as possible. We often joke about my MS if I drop something or lose at a board game! Luckily, the girls are very relaxed about it.

I still worry, feel sad, have moments of anger and can be triggered by things in day-to-day life. I have accepted that bad days are allowed and that feelings are temporary. I let myself feel however I feel and, the next day, I get up and move on. I will never be glad of my diagnosis and that is okay, but I value the lessons it has taught me, the experiences it has given me and the incredible support I have received. I can see how far I have come since I was diagnosed and how much I have changed. I have learnt how to cope, how to keep going and, more importantly, that I have an inner strength I never knew existed.

Sarah's Reflections

A lot can be said for turning on your positive thinking power. You probably know a few negative Nellies who love to dwell on the downside, lower the mood and turn everything into a pity party. They even have the ability to turn good news into something terrible by asking, "Are you sure you want to do that?" No one needs to have their bubble burst or energy zapped.

How do you turn your mind to positivity when you have been given bad news?

Give yourself a golden contract. This might sound grand, but it will change your mindset so you do not constantly feel like you need to live up to your own expectations of 'keeping face'.

Write down a handful of things that seal the deal on the golden contract with yourself. You may agree that, no matter what, you will walk the kids to school, go for a coffee with a friend, put some lipstick on, put the bins out, or just roll out of bed and take a shower. Each step to achieve little things will give you a 'sense of doing' and add back some normality.

Gratitude is everything. You may shrug this off and say, "What a load of rubbish. I'm feeling crap as I've just had the worst news of my life," but this was Anna's biggest lesson. Searching for things to be grateful for can force you to look. I would like you to stop and think. What good things have happened to allow you to reach this point in your life? Who makes your life a brilliant place to be? What do you take for granted that you may want to stop and notice?

Dial down. Can you still be happy? Absolutely. But you can also allow yourself proper 'dial down time' to switch off, wallow and be sad. It is crucial. You need to repair and heal from emotional and physical trauma. There is no time frame, each situation is unique and everyone reacts differently. Anna realised that she needed to allow herself to have bad days.

3

Gloria Battini

'No one's coming to save you' – Mel Robbins

I am now in a place where I see it with total certainty. I married a narcissist.

It took me a long time to accept that the man I had married was ruining me.

Finally, I did. Now I am free to live my life how I want.

During my school years, I was bullied. I was called 'ugly' daily and sometimes the kids would shout it across the street when I was walking home. This had a huge impact on my self-esteem, and I was never able to look in the mirror and like myself with any confidence. I grew up in a culture obsessed with looks; even my parents commented on my weight, which was hurtful and caused many arguments. In hindsight, I clearly see how the combination of these things led me to fall into the hands of someone who would later control and damage me.

When I was 18, I met a guy at a party. I was desperate to be loved and he told me everything I had always wanted to hear. I was special, I made him so much happier and I was the one he had been waiting for. I was getting attention for the first time and it felt good. I was in love.

After a few months, I noticed his strange behaviour. Certain things were not adding up. I did not like it, so I distanced myself and told him I wanted to break up. His reaction was over the top. He showered me with grand gestures, such as unexpectedly showing up to places where he knew I would be, or texting heart-wrenching words to express how much he could not live without me and promised he would change. I was naïve and he seemed genuine. That was when the deep manipulation began. All he had to do was make me feel beautiful and special and I hung on his every word. He made me believe that my friends and my mum were the bullies, and he was the only one good enough for me.

In 2009, I graduated from university and started my Masters. I met people outside my normal circle, which opened my eyes to the kind of person I was dating. I noticed more lies. He kept losing and changing jobs but it was never his fault, and I even found he had created a fake profile on Facebook. Meanwhile, my confidence was building. I felt I could start a career in events management and was looking forward to a fresh start. I was not happy and made the decision to end our relationship but, of course, he was not going to let me leave him, so the big gestures and begging went up another level. I was determined that I was not going to fall for it again but then he promised me the one thing he knew I wanted. My dream. To move to London.

During the first two years in London, he appeared responsible and hardworking. We got married in 2013 but, shortly afterwards, things turned horrible. We relocated to a small town in the countryside as he was offered a great career opportunity. I had been working my way up to become Venue Sales & Events Manager. I wanted to do well in my career but was happy to commute to support my husband. I was physically exhausted and spent many evenings on my own. He would often spend the night on the sofa with his laptop, until the early hours.

Within six months, he lost his job and demanded that we move back to London. He was letting me down again, only this time we were married and it felt much more complicated for me to leave him. I felt trapped but tried to convince him to work on our relationship and see a therapist. This is when the gaslighting started, when I was tricked into believing what was happening was normal within a marriage and that I was being overly dramatic.

My anxiety turned into an obsessive-compulsive disorder (OCD). I thought it was due to pressure at work and the long daily commute, but now know it was my way of coping with our marriage as, at least, I had some control. I withdrew from my friends and hid what was happening from everyone, including my family, as I was ashamed of my life. I had 40 rituals throughout the day; it took me an hour to leave the house and an hour to go to bed at night. He noticed my OCD but offered no support and called me crazy. In the meantime, he was jumping from job to job, sometimes unemployed for months. I somehow managed to keep things together, stayed focused on my career and became an Events Director in a new company.

Things at home continued on a downward spiral. He would blame me for my anxiety. Every time I suggested working on our marriage, he told me I was imagining things and would say, "You know how it is with us. There's a rough patch, but then we get better." When I tried to question him about our finances, I was subjected to six-hour arguments where I was left brain-blank. He would dismiss me. "You see! You don't even know why we started arguing, it's clearly not important." This continued for two years until I reached breaking point. OCD consumed me, my relationship with my mum was deteriorating and I hated myself.

By pure coincidence and lucky chance, through my work, I met a lady who was training to be a life coach, specialising in anxiety. In February 2016, I jumped at the opportunity and started some sessions with her which completely changed my life. We worked together for over three years. At first, I honestly thought my issues were around my OCD and concerns about my relationship with my mum and I remember saying to her, "Thank God I have my husband."

It is hard to understand if you have not experienced narcissistic abuse, but I believed every word he said. That it was my fault and that there was something wrong with me which had to be fixed. He never physically abused me but I was left with some huge scars, nonetheless. My life coach helped me to talk openly, and the consistent weekly sessions made me focus on what was really happening. Over time, it all started to piece together and I grew stronger. I was finally showing up for myself and could see my mindset and behaviour changing.

I knew I was evolving and ready to make big changes. I began to focus on my needs. I rediscovered my love for travel and photography. I worked on my physical health and managed to lose weight. A year later, my OCD was in a different place and life seemed lighter. My levels of anxiety began to reduce, I was able to see clearly and, through reflection, finally realised that I was suffering from trauma bonding, where I felt complete attachment and reliance on my abusive husband. Talking to a life coach made me realise that, as my parents had divorced, I was trying to ensure the same did not happen to my marriage, even if it was at the cost of my own well-being. I had always put others first and perceived that there were certain things I 'should' do to make them happy. Suddenly, I had an awareness that I must do things I wanted, that my needs were important and that I deserved better. I found my power.

Before leaving my marriage, I wanted to make sure I had tried everything to save it. After all, my inner belief was still to fight for my family. I told him I felt that we were growing apart but still wanted to save our marriage. True to form, he said that it was all in my head and it was just another phase. I asked for help from his family, but I was never supported. I was completely empty, and I knew that staying would adversely affect my health. I needed to save myself.

In January 2018, I finally made the decision, packed my bags, and walked out of a 14-year manipulative relationship (we were married for five years). Of course, he was not going to allow me to leave quietly and continued to message me for months, but I had accomplished so much in the previous two years that I felt empowered to have confidence in my decision. I knew that, by facing my problems and taking responsibility for my life, I would have the future I desperately wanted. It took a while but, in September 2019, I divorced my husband and celebrated by having a freedom dinner with my friends. It was the most amazing feeling.

We did meet up one more time and he finally confessed to knowing what he was doing. He had wanted to win and admitted feeling disappointed that my life coach had 'fixed me'. I got the closure I wanted. He tried to contact me a few more times but, eventually, it stopped.

In the following months, my relationships with friends, family, co-workers and even strangers changed as a result of my transformation. I finally believed in myself and was able to be me. I saw people differently and felt relaxed to be open about my life. A huge weight had lifted.

The worst thing about narcissistic abuse is that it is controlling and robs the victims of their identity. I could not bear the thought of other women being impacted and not having the confidence or support to break free. I wanted to do something to help others who were surviving in the shadows of their partner, feeling trapped and isolated. I started to think, 'What if all women could experience the change I have managed to bring to my life?' So, I decided to research various courses, train to become a life coach and create my own business.

I am now a Holistic coach, energy healer and psychic medium, helping people heal from a mental, emotional and spiritual point of view. I love that the career I have chosen supports women to prioritise themselves, gives them the tools to transform the way they face the world, and be confident and strong, which ultimately helps them create a different pathway.

My advice to anyone in a narcissistic relationship is to listen to your inner voice as it is your true self trying to tell you that what is going on is not right. Trust your instinct. I shut that voice down for years because I felt ashamed. Please know that there is no shame in how you are living. You have been conditioned into thinking that you are the one in the wrong.

It took a lot of work and reflection to get to this stage, but I am proud of myself. I now put myself first, know my boundaries, and recognise this is the only way I will be able to give to others. I understand my needs and they will always be my priority. I have moved from finding my coping techniques to truly being able to recognise who I am and to heal from within.

I no longer suffer from OCD. I am with a loving man and am excited for the future.

I hope this story gives you courage. Never forget that you are a gift to this world.

Sarah's Reflections

Everyone loves attention, even the wrong kind. It is easy to fall into a situation that initially feels great, and you believe is going to be good for you, but then something niggling inside makes you doubt. Suddenly you feel off-balance and your survival mode and instinct kick in.

Embrace your intuition. Gloria knew something was off. Intuition is an odd sensation that cannot be explained. It is an internal alarm bell telling you that your action or decision is questionable. Do not ignore it, as nine times out of 10 you need to pay attention. Listen and act when this alarm bell sounds. In Carl Jung's theory of the ego, he defined intuition as 'perception via the unconscious' and described an 'intuitive type acts not on the basis of rational judgement but on sheer intensity of perception'. So, either a feeling or a gut instinct.

Find a safe space. It is important to have people you can be yourself with. Normally, we can count our 'lifesavers' on one hand. Someone you like and trust, who you can share secrets with and talk openly, with no judgements, opinions or biases. We all love a friendly soothing voice, but we also need a direct approach where we are challenged. Gloria found talking to a life coach gave her the reality check and boost of confidence she needed to make changes.

A different you. If you look at yourself now, you are not the same person you were 10 years ago, a year ago or even yesterday. I love this quote from Mel Robbins, "Every phase of your life requires a different you." Gloria made a bold decision to end her marriage, which enabled her to create a different version of herself; the one she was always meant to be. Change can feel scary, which is why we often avoid it, but change can also be wonderful, liberating and necessary. Gloria has been able to find her true self, fulfil her full potential and flourish.

4
Karl Perry

'I may not have gone where I intended to go,
but I think I've ended up where I needed to be'
– Douglas Adams

I had no pulse and was not breathing.
Let's roll the story back a bit…

My wife talked me into going to A&E, where I was subsequently admitted, potentially having had a mild heart attack. I had been feeling rough for a few days, with a cold sensation in my chest when taking a deep breath. I had my own company so had soldiered on with some Lemsip, whilst managing an event we had organised. I was a reluctant patient.

I needed an angiogram but had to wait several days to be transferred to a larger hospital to do the test, which eventually concluded 'no heart attack'. As I had no symptoms and was in no pain, I was allowed to wander around the hospital in shorts and a t-shirt and was feeling fed up with missing the first BBQ of the year. However, quite by chance, they discovered that one of the main arteries to my heart was 90% blocked. It was just a little too long for a stent, so I was told they would book me in for a heart bypass, probably the following week.

That was a real blow. I was devastated. I did not know much about having a heart bypass, but I had an idea it was a tad more serious than having an ingrowing toenail. The consultant flipped my thinking by telling me I was a 'lucky man'. The blocked artery they had discovered was 'a ticking timebomb with little time left on the fuse', and it was usually, sadly, only the relatives that got to know that their loved one had a blockage.

My wife had saved my life.

There was a further two weeks of debate between surgeons as to whether a stent was still possible. The time delay was immensely frustrating as I was still symptom-free and in no pain. I was fully dressed, running errands in the hospital for other patients, and trying to fill my time. I was like Tom Hanks in *The Terminal*, stuck in my own personal *Hotel California*.

They decided on a bypass but, since I had been asymptomatic for three weeks, I was no longer a priority. It would be another three weeks before the operation, so I was discharged.

18 hours later, I had a sudden cardiac arrest (SCA).

Fortunately, my wife was at home. She phoned 999 and started CPR. I had no pulse and was not breathing. The paramedics took 11 minutes to arrive and it was only after the second shock that I was revived. My wife had saved my life for a second time. The consultants who had discharged me were at a loss as to how they had got it so wrong.

Based on movies and TV, I would have guessed that the survival rate from cardiac arrest would be quite high, maybe 70%. Alarmingly, I was advised that, for an out-of-hospital cardiac arrest (OHCA), it was 8%. And, even then, over half have brain damage and require assistance for the rest of their lives. For cardiac arrests in hospitals, with trained staff, all the oxygen, equipment and medicine immediately on hand, the survival rate is barely double.

I had been extremely lucky. I have never been that lucky. I can still barely believe it.

The operation took place within a few days. The recovery was slow and challenging. Whilst the pain relief was powerful, so were the side effects. At one point, I believed that the nurses were human-sized clicking grasshoppers, carrying out experiments on the patients. That was when I asked for my pain relief to be reduced!

Despite being almost unable to do anything during that first week, my survival instinct became intense. I do not know where it came from. Maybe it is down to evolution, but I sensed that emotions were not only irrelevant but were potentially detrimental to my recovery. I focused only on what I could do to help me progress; eat and drink, little and often, and sleep. I constantly looked for small wins. It helped me to know that I was moving in the right direction. A full and active life became my focus. I shared my goal with my consultant. I loved cycling and I was determined to be able to ride my bike in the hills again. Anything at all positive, no matter how small, was the universe telling me I was on the right path.

After a week, I was transferred from ICU into a room on a ward and, whilst the young nurse was settling me in, I said that it was a small win that I was in a side room. His reply has become a mission statement for me: "Any win's a win, and we take them all." To him, it was just a throwaway comment. To me, it went to my core. He was right. Every win should be embraced. But if we should celebrate the small wins, what should we do about the big wins? A week before, I had been dead. Now I was alive. Was there a bigger win than that?

It was only then that I realised that was the start of my second life.

The thought of a second life, a second chance, an opportunity to make refinements and do more of what made me smile and less of what did not, was a massive motivator in wanting to achieve a full recovery. I have always been a positive person. I have never been an over-the-top optimist but, certainly, I have looked for the upside in any given situation. This was a key strength in helping me handle the ups and downs of recovery. Not least, having to have a pacemaker fitted, 11 days after surgery, as my heart rate dropped to 30. I hated the thought of having a pacemaker. They were for old people who could not function. It was like being plugged into the mains and my dream of being fit and outdoorsy again was fading.

Or so I thought.

I hardly even remember I have a pacemaker now and it rarely activates. Even then, I am usually asleep. It is my safety net. My biggest concern when I was being discharged was whether I would be safe. I did not want to have to go through anything like that again. My cardiologist reassured me that he knew my heart better than his own, that everything was flowing well, and that the pacemaker was merely a precaution. He did say that sometimes the body would be ahead during recovery and, at other times, the mind. He was not wrong.

There were several key dates following my return home; Father's Day, my eldest son's birthday, getting his first car, 'A' level results and my younger son's birthday. I could not help pondering what it would be like for them if I was not there. How awful it would be. This led me to consider the possibility that there might be a parallel universe where I did not exist and my family were having an awful time. This expanded to thoughts of multiple parallel universes where I did exist but in various states of brain damage. But which one was real?

In hindsight, I should have seen a counsellor. My wife did, as she needed help to overcome the experience. I eventually counselled myself with the understanding that this was the only universe I had any influence in, so I might as well put all my emotional eggs in that basket.

Paul McGee is a motivational speaker, author of S.U.M.O. and someone I admire. He has a way of assessing situations by applying a scale of 1-10, whereby 1 is 'not much at all' and 10 is 'life-threatening'. I adapted it to 10 being 'I am dead'. I rebranded this scale as my *Shitometer*. I developed the perspective that the worst thing that could ever happen to me, had already happened. Therefore, anything else could only ever be a 9 or below. A friend described this as a superpower when making decisions. My appreciation of the numbers (there was a 92% chance that I should have died) drove my determination, and my new mission statement, into my second life to make some changes, primarily work-related.

I returned to work in September but, by December, I felt I had gone backwards. My work-life balance was non-existent and my *Shitometer* was not cutting through. I just wanted out of the events company that I had built over 15 years. I had been in talks with a senior employee for 18 months about her buying it, but I could see that it was not going anywhere. As the owner, you do not have a contract. You cannot resign. I was suffocating and feeling resentful that my second life was being taken away. My 87-year-old mum visited us over Christmas, and we unexpectedly became full-time carers. After a short decline, she died on 20th January 2020.

By 17th March 2020, I had sent my staff home due to COVID and a national lockdown was announced. All our events had to be cancelled and I knew that my business was over. I employed 12 people and, after wrapping up the refunds on all events, the last staff left in July.

At that point, I had not come to terms with my temporary death and the heart bypass, let alone started to grieve for my mum. I found myself having to get my head around my business ending as well. Thankfully my *Shitometer* began to kick in again. Many people expressed their sadness and shock at my business closure and, believe me, telling the staff it was over was my worst working day on record. But it did not match being dead.

It took me a while to realise it but, in some twisted brutal way, the universe had shown me a way out of my company. Not in the way I had wanted or would have ever wished for, but I was out. I had no idea what I was going to do with my life. Being presented with a blank canvas at 52 years of age; with no job, no company, no career and no formal training, terrified me.

It felt like the start of my third life. So, what did I do?

I cycled coast-to-coast in September 2020, raising over £5k for the hospital ward that looked after me. Sadly, and ironically, my cardiologist died of an SCA a few weeks before. His statement about knowing my heart better than his own felt prophetic. I was gutted.

I started writing everything down, just to get it out of my head. I thought that it might help with the healing process so I could try and make sense of all the events and feelings that had happened to me, as I was still playing catch-up. I captured over 110K words but it wasn't until I was two-thirds through the process that I felt things were falling into place. I had never intended to write a book but, I am proud to say, *You Only Live Thrice* has now been published.

This was a big win for me.

I began to see the blank canvas of my life as a wonderful opportunity. Something to be embraced. If we are lucky, we'll get about 80-ish orbits of the sun. This means, with a good wind, I have 25-30 summers to enjoy. It focused my mind immeasurably and irreversibly.

Perspective is a superpower.

To say that this journey has knocked me sideways does not even go near it. But being *knocked sideways* is preferable to being knocked out of the game altogether. Which, for 11 minutes, was where I was. So how can anything other than that, not be seen as an upside?

Sarah's Reflections

Perspective is one of the biggest game changers. When something goes wrong, you think, 'Why has this happened to me?' You play things back in your head, wonder if you could go back in time, or if you had chosen another option would things be better. But often you do not have a choice, so it is how you deal with it that is important. Reframing things in your mind helps you to see things differently. Karl's was, 'the worst has already happened.'

Win the day. Small wins are just as important as big wins. Karl took this valuable advice and now sees every win. It is another powerful perspective. How do you celebrate each daily win?

Scoring your life. Karl was told by a medical professional that he was 'lucky to be alive'. Statistics are scary but can give you a well-needed shake. How important is your life? Could you put a score on it? One thing that helped me, when I was at a low point, was to score my day out of 10. When you put a simple tool into practice, it can have a profound effect.

How would you score your day today?

Is there anything you could do to edge up your daily score by one point?

If you could see into the future, what would you like your score to be this time next week?

When you start to feel good enough to increase your score, you then become motivated to edge the score up a little higher, as your focus is on happiness. It then becomes self-fulfilling.

5

Anne Stephens

'It is never too late to be what you might have been'
– George Eliot

Three months after moving to Cornwall to start my dream life, a policeman knocked on my door at 10 pm, on a Sunday, and told me that my 23-year-old son had taken his own life.

It felt like a TV drama, except I did not fall to the floor weeping hysterically. Instead, I started comforting the ashen-faced policeman. It was obvious that he had not done the 'death knock' before and was finding it difficult. I found myself calmly and clinically processing the news and, bizarrely, my first thought was to cancel the chimney sweep due the next morning.

When the policeman left, I closed the door and just stood there. In that instant, the life I knew, and everything that I thought was safe, had been smashed into a million pieces. I liken it to being beaten around the head with a baseball bat, as my brain felt like mush and I could not think or breathe properly. The immense pain and anger were unbearable.

The next day, I went to autopilot. I started calling people and each one broke down crying as I spoke calmly and without emotion. A neighbour helped by making some phone calls to work and my doctor. A friend came and sat with me and my dad, and we had fish and chips. On the day Toby died, I had ordered a juicer online, and suddenly I blurted out, "Would it be terrible if I went to Argos and collected my juicer?"

When I look back, I still cannot tell you why I was not a crumbling heap on the floor. I know I was in shock. But what should a grieving mother look like? A pale tear-stained face with no make-up or smile? There were days I cried and howled but, if anyone saw me on the street, they would never have guessed that I had just experienced the worst tragedy of my life.

I had to deal with so much in a short space of time. I drove from Cornwall to Cambridge where Toby had lived when he died, met the policeman who had found him, went to see my son's body and arranged his funeral. I then went back to Cornwall and just carried on. I even went online and bought a puppy, as something deep inside me knew I needed to find a reason to go on. Toby's funeral was held in Cambridge, so

I travelled back again. The day after I returned to Cornwall, my dad was diagnosed with terminal cancer. I felt numb.

Toby was a headstrong stubborn child, who was fiercely independent and chose his friends carefully. He was highly intelligent but his school exam results did not reflect his intellect as, like many bright young men, he struggled to stay motivated about things he found boring. As an only child, he had learned to entertain himself with computer games. In his teens, and up to when he died, playing online with people all over the world was a huge part of his life. I brought Toby up as a single parent and worked full-time to support us. I found it a struggle at times but had help from my parents, and I did my best to give him a good life.

After a few false starts at trying to hold down a job, Toby decided he wanted to go to university. He started a degree in computing and, in the first year, he seemed to thrive as he made new friends and lived in Halls. In Year 2, he seemed to go off the rails, as he went into a shared house and started to miss lectures and play computer games instead. He just appeared to lack motivation. I then discovered that he had dropped out of university, which meant that he had to come home to live with me.

It got to the point, when Toby was 23, that I felt I had to let him live his own life and it was time for me to follow my dreams. I had always wanted to move to Cornwall. My aunt lived there; we went every summer when I was a child and I had always felt drawn back. I took Toby there on holiday many times when he was little and we had happy times together. I was 55 and had just broken up with the man I thought I would spend the rest of my life with when I took the huge leap and quit my IT job, sold my house and moved to Cornwall with my dad. I told Toby that he could come too, but he chose to stay in Cambridge to be near his friends. I said I would continue to support him while he figured his life out.

I spoke to Toby on the phone the week he died and nothing seemed wrong, other than normal young man worries. There were no clues and his friends were as shocked as I was – it came totally out of the blue. The police gave me some of his belongings and I discovered, from notes he had made, that he had planned when he was going to take his life.

Shortly after Toby's funeral, I was in the garden with my puppy Elfie and found myself looking up to the sky, silently crying out for help. At that moment, I had an epiphany - I saw three clear choices in front of me. The first was to take all the diazepam the doctor had prescribed and walk into the sea. The second was to live every moment of my remaining life in misery and pain and the third choice was that I could find a way to live the best life I possibly could. Nothing would change what had happened, Toby was not coming back.

The loss of a child is so deep and suicide loss comes with a whole layer of other complex emotions. You often think about them and the future that you were supposed to witness. The constant question of why, the guilt, the stigma – all these were yet to come but, at that time, making the third choice was my first step. I had no idea how, but I knew I was going to find a way to live again and maybe even feel happy. I thought this was what Toby would have wanted. I do not believe he had wanted to cause me pain. He probably thought he was a burden. Maybe he thought it was for the best. My only salvation was that I was living in Cornwall. I could not have been in a better place to start my long healing journey.

When Toby was 18, I turned 50 and started on a personal development journey, as I felt it was time to focus on myself. I attended seminars, hired a life coach and read countless books on how to change your mindset and improve your life. I strongly believe that what I had learned equipped me with tools to help me control how I reacted and move forward.

When someone dies suddenly, and unexpectedly, there is an inquest into their death. It is an open hearing; anyone can attend, and you usually find young reporters hanging around, waiting for any gory details that might make headlines. After the inquest, I chose to speak to the journalists as I wanted them to tell my story. A few weeks later, the newspaper contacted me to ask if I could write a story for their weekend section. This was how I started writing about my loss and I found it therapeutic, which led me to begin a blog about my recovery.

I went to my GP, to seek support, but they were no help at all and did not signpost me to any organisations, so I set about searching myself. With my dad dying from cancer, I felt utterly alone in my grief. I tried the Samaritans, and they would listen but I wanted much more. I needed to believe that it would get better. I needed advice and connection from someone who understood, to make me feel I would survive. I found an organisation in the UK called Survivors of Bereavement by Suicide (SOBS), which had a helpline and ran support groups. I called the helpline a lot. Everyone at the end of the phone had been bereaved by suicide, but I found that I could only relate to other parents who had lost a child.

Searching the internet, I found groups for parents who had experienced the loss of a child, although not specifically by suicide. Through this, I knew I needed to connect with parents who had the same experience as me and, with some help from a friend, I set up my own support group on Facebook called *Losing a Child to Suicide UK*. From my experience, when you are going through hell, the first thing you need is someone to let you know that you are not alone. I have had parents tell me that my support group has saved their lives. There is nothing more valuable than that, and it has also helped me to cope better.

I continued my blog and was asked to become a trustee for a charity that works to prevent young suicide. I have been on TV and radio, trying to raise awareness of young suicide and let people know what support is out there. In hindsight, I did too much in that first year. My dad died four months after Toby, and I was left alone and lost. I threw myself into finding a job, campaigning and started a counselling course in the evenings. Looking back, I do not know how I did it all – I just kept going.

I tried counselling but talking about Toby left me sobbing and feeling like I killed him, by being an overbearing mum who leapt to his rescue every time he needed help. Instead, I found that joining a choir and a walking group helped me the most, as I met people who did not know my sad story and I could feel normal and tell them later when I felt ready.

Strangely, losing Toby made me focus as it allowed me to become selfish and realise what I wanted and needed out of life. I became determined to find some meaning in the tragedy, as I wanted to make sure his death would not feel pointless. I wanted to shout out and warn other parents that, out of the blue, their child could take their own life.

I like to think Toby would have wanted me to live a good life.

I live a good life in his memory and aim to honour him. I went to university three years after Toby died and did a degree in journalism. I got a first and wrote my dissertation on how the media report on suicide. On my 60th birthday, I did a trek in the Sahara Desert and raised £4,000 for a charity that works to prevent young suicide.

I lost Elfie a few years ago, but now have two wonderful rescue dogs who keep me going on dark days. I joined a choir and found that singing for two hours a week was a welcome release and it helped me to heal. I still write my blog and plan to turn it into a book one day. I will continue to support other parents, who have lost their child to suicide, in raising awareness and stopping the stigma. The statistics of suicide in young adults is shocking, especially for young men, and I want to do everything I can to help reduce it.

Toby was my only child, my world, my everything. It has been 12 years since my beautiful son died. I know it was not my fault and that suicide is complicated. I also know I will always feel heartache for the loss of my son, but I want to ensure that I live the best life possible.

Sarah's Reflections

I cried when I first heard Anne's story. As a parent, I caught a glimpse of how heartache feels.

You always have a choice. Anne speaks openly about the three options available to her. It is essential to understand that the choice to live your life the best way possible is in your hands. Anne will always miss her son, she has sad days and bad days, but she has a zest for life and wants to ensure that she can continue to live in memory of her beautiful boy, Toby.

The right connection. It may feel like a scattergun approach at first but it is vital, when dealing with grief, that you find people who understand. Anne explained the difference it had made to her to speak to other parents who had lost a child to suicide. When you find the right connection, you do not have to explain as they already know how you feel. There is an added comfort with no awkwardness or tiptoeing around a topic that others will avoid. When you share, and learn ways of coping, it can give you reassurance there is a way out of the darkness.

Power of purpose. Doing small things can help you move forward after a significant loss. There is no time frame, there are no rules, but having a small distraction is often necessary. Anne found singing and walking lifted her spirits the most. Anne also found purpose by focusing on helping other parents and raising awareness of suicide in young adults.

6
Paola Palmieri

'Vulnerability is not weakness, it's our most accurate measure of courage' – Brene Brown

My husband, sister and I sat in the oncologist's office and heard the word 'cancer'. Not the type that makes you go through hell and come out victorious at the end to ring the golden bell. I had the one they call incurable; stage 4 or, if you want to be a jerk about it, terminal.

It is safe to say that this takes the cake for life's hard hits.

Before my diagnosis, I remember thinking, "Why is it that nothing bad ever happens to me?" There are so many people suffering from difficult situations, and I felt that I had a perfect life. I had a great childhood with loving parents and an entire family support system. I went to college, graduated, moved to the city of my dreams, met an incredible person whom I married and then had two beautiful healthy boys. We lived in a nice apartment near the beach, my husband had a good job, I adored my job working part-time as a college professor, and life could not get any better. I had it all figured out and everything was going according to plan.

It was in the middle of all this perfection that my body was trying to tell me something. I started having strange symptoms; chronic diarrhoea, night sweats and heart palpitations that felt like anxiety attacks. This went on for a couple of years. I dismissed all these symptoms as gluten intolerance or hormonal imbalances after having children. One day, I decided to listen to my body and made an appointment to see a gastroenterologist. She ordered tests which I took my time to get done because, in my mind, it was still not a big deal. 6 months later, I got the results. "They could be blood vessels, but the radiologist thinks it is cancer."

The doctor referred me to an oncologist, but I remember thinking, "I can't possibly have cancer. This is insane. I am one of the most active and healthy people I know." The news was shocking, to say the least. I made the appointment with the oncologist and, a few days later, a biopsy confirmed my worst nightmare. "You have stage 4 cancer."

As soon as that word came out of his mouth, we gripped our hands tighter and we all held our breath. This doctor had an interesting way of delivering the news.

"I have good and bad news. The bad news is that it IS cancer. The good news is that it's a good cancer. It is called Neuroendocrine cancer. You have a primary tumour in your small bowel that is inoperable due to its location, and it has metastasized (spread) to your liver. You have innumerable tumours in your liver, but you are going to live a long time."

Say that again. What the hell is a good cancer? Although it made no sense to me, I was extremely happy to hear that it was not all bad. But I still did not understand how there could be anything 'good' about a stage 4 incurable cancer. Was he aware that there is no stage 5?

After the diagnosis, we discussed the plan of action which involved having a monthly injection of a synthetic hormone to manage the symptoms and keep the tumours stable. We also talked about seeking a specialist's opinion and going over the many treatment options. I honestly left the hospital jumping up and down. I was the happiest newly diagnosed cancer patient. I almost felt bad that I had it so good. The treatment sounded a piece of cake and I felt just fine, despite a few symptoms. I quickly came to realise that, once you enter the world of cancer, it can become all-consuming. Knowing I had an advanced 'good' cancer even started to take its toll on my well-being. Now in hindsight, I do not feel that there is such a thing as a 'good' cancer, and I believe healthcare professionals should never refer to it in this way. When you first hear the diagnosis and then go through treatment, cancer is cancer, and it sucks just the same.

I constantly think about my future and what life has in store for me.

My diagnosis has been quite a learning experience. During the first year after my diagnosis, cancer used to be my first and last thought every day. I would wake up and say to myself, "Yeah, I still have cancer." I would cry when talking to my mom on the phone, telling her how much I hated having it and how much I wanted it to go away. I had to constantly worry about staying alive for my children because the thought of not being able to watch them grow would eat me up inside. I dealt with four rounds of an intense treatment called liver embolisation to debulk the tumour load in my liver. I have to have a monthly subcutaneous shot with an 18-gauge needle in my butt that leaves everlasting lumps. I still get anxious about scans and I think this will continue to be part of my life, as I endure the wait to hear the results.

Thankfully, I have received positive news after all my scans and for now, other than my monthly injection, there is no need for additional therapies or treatments. When the time comes for a new treatment, I know I will be able to handle it. I have been training to face this evil, conniving and deadly enemy. I feel prepared and ready. Bring it on, stupid cancer.

When I speak about being prepared to face more cancer therapies, I think of it as getting my body and mind ready. The moment I heard that I had incurable cancer, I thought there had to be a way for me to have some control over it. In the following weeks, I read about patients beating cancer through nutrition and natural holistic approaches. These remarkable stories sparked my interest, and I threw myself into finding out as much as possible. Armed with newfound knowledge, I found hope and this encouraged me to start my own healing journey.

The first step was thinking of food as medicine and eating with purpose. I removed red meat from my diet, followed by all other meat and, eventually, fish. I had learnt that protein can be found in plant-based foods and, in some cases, in even higher proportions. In the following few months, I decided to cut out dairy products and became a vegan. I juiced vegetables and fruit every morning, drank 60 ounces of water daily, and made sure I added superfoods, and other supplements, to my meals. I focused on anti-inflammatory and liver-cleansing foods, foods low in amines and with anti-cancer properties which helped with bloating and gave me a healthy digestion. Food became my way to thrive. All the meals I ate served a purpose and, with every bite, I felt more and more empowered. The change in my diet by no means replaced my treatments and therapies. This was in addition, as I felt they could work well together and allowed me to have some control over my diagnosis.

I knew that healing involves the mind as well as the body. During the first year after my diagnosis, my thoughts were too loud, complicated, dark and disruptive. I needed to quiet them down somehow. I started working on short, guided meditation sessions following YouTube videos, downloaded a couple of apps and took some meditation classes. My favourite event was the full moon beach meditation as it felt like a surreal experience that gently helped me open my heart and dig deep inside myself. Meditation helped clear my head, calm my nerves, focus on the present and allow me to appreciate the moment. I also started practising breathing techniques, which are especially helpful during scan days. Meditation has become a daily routine for me. I spend 10 to 15 minutes sitting still, while breathing and acknowledging my thoughts but not clinging to them.

Another essential aspect of thriving with cancer is staying active. I have always been an active person. I love exercising, dancing, yoga and running. Exercise has helped me feel empowered. I think of it as giving my body the tools to make me feel strong, determined and accomplished. "Fuck you, cancer. I am stronger than you!" Luckily, I have been able to continue my exercise routine without too many restrictions. My yoga practice is the one activity that became a priority after my diagnosis. It has helped me connect with my body. I listen to it and pay attention to what it is trying to tell me. This practice fulfils my physical needs, as well as my spiritual curiosity, as it teaches me something new every time. I set myself a challenge to learn as much as I could about yoga, and I have recently registered for a yoga teaching program. I am thrilled that I can follow through with this goal.

I would always encourage people to take life by the horns. Whether you are going through cancer, or any other challenging situation, there are times in life when we get a wake-up call and we must make changes. These horrible things happen to make us realise what our priorities in life should be. If cancer had not happened to me, I think I would still be bothered by trivial things and not give those who matter the quality time they deserve. I would rarely stop to appreciate a beautiful sunset or sunrise or take the time to really feel the softness of my children's hands inside mine. I am in no way saying that I am happy or blessed to have cancer. Trust me, I would much rather not, but I do appreciate the lessons I have learned. As far as my prognosis, I do not have the answer to that. Thankfully I have not been given an expiration date and my doctors have said that I can live a long time. I am not sure what 'long' means to them but, for me, it means the world. Long enough to make the best of it. I am feeling healthier and stronger than ever and, while I still suffer from anxiety, especially before my scans which are every eight months, I manage to work around it.

Life knocked me sideways when I was told that I had incurable cancer at the age of 37. I felt as if my world was crumbling down. I could not see myself celebrating that year's holidays, participating in buying a new house with my family or even just being present in my children's lives. I kept calculating the number of years the treatments would be successful and giving myself an expiration date. I realised that I could not live my life that way. It was not fair to me, or my family, to have that kind of perspective, so I made changes.

I now feel that it is possible to live a happy and healthy life with cancer. This major curveball has taught me more than I could have ever imagined. I love life fiercely and take my chances. I laugh harder, cry more often, and love more passionately. I create memories that my loved ones will not forget. I live with purpose and, while I may not become a grandmother (or maybe I will), I know I have given my best to my life. My biggest hope is that my children will have great memories and will have learned how to fully live.

After all, this is the reason we are all here – to be alive and, more importantly, FEEL alive!

Sarah's Reflections

When I chatted with Paola over Zoom, I immediately felt her passion and determination.

She was given news that really shook her world, but she was not about to give up.

Control your destiny. Never give up on life, as there is still so much on offer. Paola made the decision to take control and give herself a fighting chance. Often, people can sit back and let life happen to them, but you are capable of so much more. You are in the driving seat.

Essential health choices. Paola made changes to her life which improved her long-term diagnosis. To live a healthy life, you need to find the right balance of physical and mental well-being. NHS England describes diet, exercise, hydration and sleep as essential. Try not to make drastic changes, and immediately give up everything you consider bad, as that will make you unhappy. Make minor adjustments and be aware of how they support your long-term health.

Do not sweat the small stuff. Paola's wake-up call made her realise where her priorities needed to be. You can get tied up in knots over trivial things when, in truth, you need to let them go. If you step back and count from 1 to 10, it will slow down your reactions so you can see what is important. This will do wonders to strip away unwanted stress and anxiety.

7
Emma Morgan

'She needed a hero, so that's what she became'
– Anonymous

It was a rainy Sunday afternoon when my marriage ended. It was like the death of a relative who has been ill for some time, where you keep hoping they will pull through and see another day. I was in a café and got the news over text, quite simply put 'I can't do this anymore'. Our short marriage, of just four years, had been in trouble for a while and similar threats to end it, from both sides, had been made. I just knew, this time, that he meant it.

I felt like I had been punched.

I did not know what to do. Should I go home or just head out and start walking in whatever direction my feet took me? I opted for home and, when I arrived, my husband was packing his bags to stay in a hotel for the night. That first night was the loneliest I have ever felt in my life. I did not want to tell anyone, so I put my son to bed, sat alone and sobbed. I waited to get a message to say it was a huge mistake, that we were better than that, but it never came.

The early days were difficult. I struggled to tell people that we were splitting up without breaking down in tears. I told everyone I knew, in the most removed way possible, via a Facebook status update. I cringe now remembering it but, at the time, it felt the easiest way of letting everyone know all at once. Even telling my close family and friends felt too much, so I sent a wave of messages and said I would talk to them in person once I felt I could hold a conversation. It was a long time before I felt able to say, "My marriage is over," aloud.

After that initial milestone, the next few weeks saw me in survival mode. I went into automatic pilot and vowed to myself to keep the show on the road for my son. In fact, if it was not for him, I am not sure I would have made it out of bed. I was grateful to see his beautiful baby moon face greet me every morning. He was the main reason to keep going.

Work was both a saviour and a challenge. I had recently started a new role but, whilst I was still thrilled by that, it felt like a cloud hanging over my head. I cannot think of many more awkward conversations to have with a new line manager, but having to explain that your marriage had just ended is definitely up there. I got amazing support and I am still grateful that I had the space to talk, as elsewhere I was keeping most of the details to myself.

There is a song by Kate Bush called *This Woman's Work* and it describes perfectly how those first few weeks felt. The line 'I should be crying but I just can't let it show' was how I felt around family and friends, particularly my parents. I did not want them to worry, so I put on a brave face while deep inside I was the most lost I had ever felt in my life. The song talks about regrets for what should have been said and done; and the blame she assigned to herself for the downfall. It was as if Kate had looked inside my mind and turned my thoughts into lyrics. I am not sure that a song has ever spoken to me in such a way, and I would often play it to release my melancholy as I grieved, like a teenager, for my failed relationship.

My lowest moment came about a week after the split. I got confirmation that my husband was moving on and I felt alone and in despair. The realisation of him finding someone else hurt more than the rejection when he told me that our marriage was over. I sat in bed, feeling like I was living a nightmare, listening to the same radio talk show I had listened to for years. The familiar sounds of the presenters' voices soothed me and kept the tears at bay with their light-hearted chatter and requests to call in. Almost trance-like, I dialled the number and, within minutes, I found myself on air, sharing personal woes about my marriage ending. The kindness of strangers helped me get through another angry confrontation with my husband when he got in from work later that night. I did not sleep well. The next day, I listened to my radio replay and was sad to hear a meek and broken soul on the line. I wept, knowing that voice was mine. Then came my 'aha' moment as I started to listen more intently.

The radio presenter said, "You know, the thing about breakups is that someone nearly always comes off worse and I'm sorry to say but, in this case, I think that's you." I do not know why, but that was the verbal shove I needed. I knew he was right, but it did not have to be like that forever.

From that moment, I started to rebuild myself and get to grips with this new part of my life. I focused on small things, like getting the basics right. I made sure I showered, got my toddler up and ready for nursery, commuted into work and got home. The tears became less frequent as I started to gain confidence at work, and I slowly accepted my new identity.

By far the hardest part was the limbo period of living together and waiting for my husband to find somewhere else. I did not think that the atmosphere in our home could get much worse than the build-up to our split, but I was wrong. We were reacting in very different ways. I had gone insular and wanted to hide from the world, whereas my husband was on a quest for freedom from a marriage he feared being trapped in forever, and his relief was clear. As I was grieving, he appeared to be reborn, and that difference brought its own conflicts and frustrations. We lived together for a long six months. There were turbulent days, but we mostly tried to keep out of each other's way. Although it meant the end, I was keen for him to leave as I knew I could not start to move on with my life while we were still under one roof.

I began to run as a way of escape. This was as much a surprise to me as anyone since I had always declared I could not run. What I loved, right from the start, was the space it gave me away from the house. It had become more like a prison than a home. While running, I had many lightbulb moments, mainly from songs I listened to. I have always found music to be good for my soul and I often use it to soothe anxious thoughts and inspire me. Lyrics often resonate. One of the most impactful was from Lizzo's *Good as Hell*, 'If he doesn't love you anymore, walk your fine ass out the door.' I remember sprinting the final stretch as those words sank in. It was a powerful moment as I realised that I needed to start getting over my loss.

Then the day arrived that I had dreaded and longed for in equal measure; the day he moved out. More tears and my inner critic raged in my head that I would never cope on my own as a single mum. I was convinced that I would sink and fail. But I didn't. I took things a day at a time and, steadily, built myself back up. I had fun with my son and even went on a date or two. Then lockdown came, with many challenges, but I faced them with my son and we now make a formidable team. There is another lyric in *This Woman's Work* that sang out louder to me than others. I barely paid it any attention but, as I accepted my new life, the words got louder and louder each time I listened, 'I know you've got a little life in you left, I know you've got a lotta strength left.' The more time passed, the more I believed I did have life left in me. It was at that moment I decided I would do more than just survive. I was going to thrive in my new life.

I yearned to do something creative relating to my experience and I also felt drawn to help anyone going through a divorce or having marriage difficulties. I wanted to create a comforting beacon, a small light in other people's dark moments. It would allow me to share my experiences and feelings and give hope and support to others in need. That was how my podcast *The Crazy Ex Club* was born. I started season one and recorded an episode a week, covering different aspects of how to rebuild yourself, and your life, following a breakup. This has evolved into an interview podcast and, each week, a different person talks about a breakup they have overcome. The purpose of the show is to help people see that they are not alone. So many others understand, having been through the same, and got out the other side.

I am a big believer in the power of community when working through problems, so I created a coaching course called *How to Survive Your Breakup*. This is aimed at people who need support in rebuilding their lives after a breakup, by learning the steps to survive the first stages and then reconnect with themselves, so they can build goals and a life they are excited about. The main ethos behind *The Crazy Ex Club* is to 'push forward with kindness', as this has been my personal driving force. If I can help one person discover that being a 'Crazy Ex' might be the best thing that can ever happen to them, then I am on the right track.

I have started to share content on TikTok to extend the audience and spread the message of *The Crazy Ex Club* community even further. I am currently working towards the day when I can take the subject to a live event. This just shows how my confidence has grown.

After a two-year separation, our divorce was finalised. It was emotional, but I am extremely hopeful for my future. As desperate as I felt when my marriage ended, the feelings have passed, and it has led me to become the most independent and authentic version of myself. For that, I am grateful. I am pleased to say that things have remained amicable. We co-parent as best we can and even swap dating tales over a cup of tea every now and then.

Now I feel fearless as I have stopped worrying about what people think. I get out there and do the things I want to do. If the breakup has changed me in any way, it is to have more faith in myself and what I can achieve. I had to face one of my biggest fears head on and I have come out the other side, smiling and feeling proud. If anyone reading this is going through something similar, just know that you have got this. Everything is going to be all right.

Sarah's Reflections

Your zing is the best thing. For many reasons, you can lose yourself. You get stuck in a situation without even realising; busyness, commitments and general life admin can make you forget who you are. What things do you value? What do you want to achieve? What things light you up? Emma discovered a new identity which allowed her to find her zing again.

Rhythm of routine. When you deal with adversity, you may have to use every inch of willpower to get out of bed and go through the motions of daily life. Emma knew that her son's needs were her priority and work became her lifeline. Routine offers safety. You have a routine to follow which gets you from A to B, often without realising. I know how discombobulated (I love that word) I feel if my routine is out of whack. How you use your hours each day is essential. Break tasks into manageable chunks, do not over-commit and ensure that you have 'you time'. I discovered the amazing book

The Miracle Morning by Hal Elrod, which is an essential part of my daily routine. I allow myself 30 minutes to meditate, journal and read. This has helped me to focus, declutter my head and start the day well.

Words change worlds. Emma found a connection to lyrics that helped her recognise and deal with her emotions. Music is a wonderful way to express and interpret how you feel. I bet you have a favourite song and know all the words and hearing it reminds you of a time, place or person. It can be enriching to connect, escape and let go, even for five minutes. And if you are feeling extra brave you could even sing aloud, which will offer a welcome release.

8

Fiona Myles

'Endurance produces character and character produces hope' – Romans 5, verse 4

I had catapulted myself from one disaster to the next and my life had hit rock bottom.

In 1995 I was in hospital for the fourth time, having had another seizure due to the amount of alcohol and drugs in my system. My daily routine was to wake up, smoke weed, drink vodka and snort speed to end the evening. At 29 years old, my body was shouting at me to stop.

As I lay there waiting for the doctor, I started to think about the first time I had taken drugs.

I was 17, homeless and sleeping in Victoria Station in London after being chucked out of my latest failed nanny position in Borehamwood. Some of the street-sleepers were smoking weed and I started to show an interest as they were all laughing and having a great time. One of the older guys had a guitar and some were singing folky-type songs, so I sat down alongside them. When the joint came around, I took a draw. It was so strong on the back of my throat that I thought I was going to cough my guts up. A young girl called Danielle laughed and explained how to do it better for the next time. That was the beginning of my addiction.

I was an adopted kid with a big chip on my shoulder. Abandonment issues, rejection and fear constantly filled my mind. As a mixed-up 14-year-old, I had attempted to murder my sister as I resented her being my parents' birth child. In my troubled mind I thought that, if I got rid of her, I might be loved more. I put a carrier bag over her head and tried to suffocate her in the middle of the night. Thankfully, she struggled and I let go. I had an awful temper and caused no end of trouble, so my parents were glad to wave me off when I was 16.

I was from a little village in Scotland, so London seemed an amazing place. Eventually, after my stint sleeping on the streets, I moved into a DHSS hotel which I thought was great. I became good friends with Danielle who had her own troubles but seemed nice. It was sad that I had to leave her behind suddenly. One night, I ran away from the flat where we had been set up to 'entertain' smelly old men. The awful fear after being raped was just too much.

I lurched into another set of people who I thought were great until I didn't do as I was told. That night, I was beaten so badly that I lost my 20-week-old baby boy who I did not know I was carrying. Like a wounded animal, I limped off to find solace in a different part of town.

I became attached to another new crowd. They were into Acid in a big way. I loved tripping out and enjoyed how my mind conjured up different images. I shacked up with the drug dealer. An older girl talked me into stealing his drugs. That did not go well, as I was caught. I found myself held in a room as he threatened to kill me. I managed to escape and another guy I knew allowed me to hide in his room. I prefer not to think about those memories.

I ended up in Southern Ireland with the guy who saved me from being killed. We smoked weed, sang songs and became real hippies. It was 1985 and Band Aid was the highlight of the year. Things were going well. We got married and moved to Glasgow. Then he started drinking excessively and developed a nasty temper. When matched with mine, it caused violent moments. Life suddenly did not feel so good. I had been through so much and my mind was full of memories I could not cope with. Drugs and alcohol numbed everything.

We had only been married for two years when we split for a while. I missed him, although it was a relief to be away from the tension. I then decided it was the right time to search for my natural family. I knew they lived in London, so that was a good place to start. We got back together a few months later and he agreed to help me find my parents. Sadly, my most stark memory from that time was when I discovered he had been unfaithful several times.

Utterly defeated, I skulked off back to Scotland on my own, where my aunt let me stay in her flat, on the 21st floor of a tower block in Glasgow. I was sad, lonely and angry. Surviving each day consisted of sleeping and drinking. It all came to a head one night when I tried to take my own life. I was only 21. So much had happened in such a short space of time and I did not know how to go on anymore. I climbed out onto the balcony ledge of the flat and pushed myself off. But, by some fluke, I landed back on the balcony in complete shock.

I then rented a flat in Govan where I met husband number two. He was selling drugs next door. We got on well and, overall, I thought he was a nice guy. When I was 25, we got married and decided to get out of Glasgow and move to Falkirk. My life with him followed the same pattern; getting high, followed by arguments, and then making up.

Rolling back to where my chapter began, my hospital visits were becoming too frequent. The doctor came to talk to me with a stern look on his face. The seizures were due to my body not coping with 13 years of bad habits. He told me clearly that I may not be so lucky next time

and I needed to review my life. As I left the hospital, everything felt different. I was scared and fully aware of the damage I was doing. I did not want to die. Things had to change, but I had learned to survive by drinking alcohol and taking drugs. I did not think I could cope without them.

Tragedy struck my family as my sister's baby boy was stillborn due to spina bifida. My head was spinning. My sister was a kind person, so why would something like that happen? The church had been a great support to her during that awful heartache. She asked me to go, on her behalf, to say thank you to the minister. I remember thinking that there was no way a person like me, with a list of sins, would be allowed in but I did my duty by my sister.

I started to think about my own mortality. Thoughts of dying and questions about life after death came to the forefront of my mind. This seemed to trigger something in me and slowly I began reducing my drug and alcohol intake, as I knew they were damaging me.

A few weeks later, a neighbour invited me to her church. I accepted the offer and went with her one Sunday night. I was surprised by how lively it was. I remember thinking that it was quite good and not boring or uncomfortable like the church I had gone to for my sister.

The next time I visited the church was a few months later. We had just lost our twins after going through IVF. We had tried for many years to have a baby, with no luck, having been told it was unexplained infertility. Losing our babies was devastating. Up to that point, I had no faith and did not believe in God, but I experienced something real in the church that day and suddenly things began to change. I was determined to make my life better because, for the first time in years, I felt a tiny sliver of hope. Bit by bit, I was able to start untangling everything. People prayed for me and were kind and helpful, which had never happened to me before. Instead of filling my body with drugs and alcohol, my time was filled with prayer, reading the Bible and other books that helped me to heal, both mentally and emotionally.

As time went on, I began to grow in my new-found faith in Jesus. Unfortunately, my husband did not feel the same and, after a brief affair with a local woman who became pregnant with his child, he said he was leaving me. I found myself homeless yet again but, this time, I had people who rallied around to help me. I rented a house and began living life with my new-found faith. I felt it was important to start helping other women, so I opened my home. Many came to talk with me, and some even moved in until they found their feet. Each of the women had their own set of troubles and I poured out the love that had been shown to me when I first found the church and developed my faith in God.

A few years later, I met and married the most wonderful man who was 13 years my junior. He had been a heroin addict and had found faith in Jesus too. Together, we managed a house where women came to live for a year to get off drugs or alcohol. We saw many women make significant changes, turn their lives around and be reunited with their families.

After 10 years of marriage, we still had no children. I had been to a religious conference, a few years earlier, and had heard from God that I would have a child when I was 50. I could not see how that would happen as I had started the menopause a couple of years previously. I had fantasised that one of the women we worked with would leave a baby on the doorstep. Not being able to have children had been such a strain on my previous marriages. Always getting the same answer after endless invasive hospital tests. I had thought that being clean and in a stable loving marriage, would help me conceive but, years later, there was still no baby. I must have used at least a thousand pregnancy tests over the years.

I then found out that my great-niece, who had some health issues, was going to be taken into care. After rigorous assessments, we were deemed fit to become her guardians. She was placed in our care six weeks before my 51st birthday. She became the apple of our eye and the promise that God had given us. I stood up in the pulpit and told the whole church what I believed God had said to me. Some knew how many years I had yearned for a child. Our marriage continues to be strong, and we have weathered many trying times together.

I believe there is always hope.

To the addict, you can get clean. To those yearning for a child, it may not be the way that you have imagined, but perhaps start to think differently. My faith had a lot to do with my turnaround in life. I built a relationship with God, and He made a way for me to find my freedom and to have the desire of my heart.

Our little girl, Georgie, is now eight years old. She has complex needs as her tummy mummy was an addict. She was born addicted to drugs and alcohol and had a brain bleed when she was one day old, which resulted in developmental problems.

Georgie is my pure delight. A force to be reckoned with and full of energy and fun. She is not easy to manage but I have learnt so much through her and she brings huge waves of joy to our lives. Who would have thought that a hopeless pair of drug addicts would be entrusted with a gorgeous little pocket rocket who also started life with a drug addiction?

It is amazing how life can turn out.

Sarah's Reflections

Fiona's younger years were full of turmoil and she was close to not surviving. It is clear from reading her story that she is determined, resilient and strong. But where does that come from?

Who are you? Identity holds a lot of meaning. It is important to take time to know who you are. Many factors play a significant role in shaping your sense of self and how you relate to others. Genetics can dictate our behaviour, but our own will and how we experience life events are also big factors. Fiona struggled to know her identity, which caused her extreme internal pain. When she felt a sense of belonging, her journey of self-discovery began.

Finding a community is a fundamental part of living. A place where you feel you belong. Some find family their biggest comfort, while others have an amazing network of friends. Work can be where you spend most of your time, so these relationships can blossom. Fiona found her community in God and the church, where she could be herself and feel valued and accepted.

Pay it forward. Many featured in this book have drawn upon their experiences to make a difference to others, which creates a ripple effect and spreads the kindness wider. In Fiona's case she talked about opening her house to support other women. When your focus is projected outward it can be the shift you need away from your own problems, which will have the biggest impact on how you feel inward. Showing kindness is wonderful and, as an added bonus, boosts your sense of self-worth.

9

Etya Vaserman Krichmar

'To live is to suffer, to survive is to find some meaning in the suffering' – Friedrich Nietzsche

My first encounter with anti-Semitism happened on a frosty winter morning in Kotovsk, Ukraine, when I was nine years old. My family had just moved into our first government-owned apartment, which my parents had waited 30 years to receive approval for. I later learnt that the long wait had everything to do with quotas and their Jewish identity.

In anticipation of meeting some children and making new friends, I woke up early, eager to explore the neighbourhood. Expecting an adventure, I quickly devoured my breakfast and put on warm clothes. The heavy blue coat felt snug and, layered on top, I wore a large babushka, a hand-knitted 'plátok', big enough to cover my head and the rest of little me. Mama had wrapped it around my coat by crisscrossing its extended, protruding ends and tying them firmly behind my back. She wanted to make sure I had the extra protection against the weather. The winters in Ukraine can be brutal because the average temperatures are below freezing. Mama's act of kindness turned me into a living stuffed doll. It restricted my movement but did not stop me from going out. On my feet I wore 'valenki', which are winter boots made of boiled wool. They kept my feet warm and my legs from slipping as I walked through freshly fallen snow. Most Russians wore them without minding how bulky, stiff and ugly they were. I walked with determination, through the piles of crisp snow, on my quest to find some friends.

At that moment, everything seemed okay in my world. The reflections from the sun's rays created a myriad of colours. Feeling curious and brave, enjoying the picture-perfect scenery and pretending to be in a winter wonderland, I came across a group of children my age. I noticed they each had a snowball and were about to build a snowman. I wanted to play too, and here was my chance to make new friends. Expecting to have fun, I ran towards them but, as soon as I approached, I heard the creak from an open window and a woman's loud voice yelling, "Don't play with her. This girl is a Kike!"

Hearing those words, the children scattered. I froze. Alone, dumbfounded and hurt, I stood there. The excitement I had felt left me and, instead, the feeling of dread held me in its grip. In that instant, my life changed. Without knowing the reason, I felt defeated. Being so young, I could not understand what the word 'Kike' meant but I strongly felt the pain of rejection. It was dreadful.

Distraught, I turned around and hurried back home with tears flowing down my cheeks. Sobbing and heaving, I told Mama what had happened. She wiped away my tears, held me close in a tight embrace, and stroked my back to make me feel calm. Only when I stopped crying did she tell me that we were Jewish. She then explained the ugly meaning of the word 'Kike'. The hateful word that the woman had used to describe me to the other children.

Reminiscing puts things in a new perspective. As I look back at the events that took place on that beautifully pristine winter morning, I realise I lost my innocence that day. The woman had killed it with hate and buried it in the pile of snow. Decades later, I carry no ill feelings towards those children because, like me, they were the victims of circumstance. It was not their fault, but the generational prejudice that spoke through the crack of the open window. Years have passed and I have forgiven my abusers, even those who were adults and intentionally wanted to belittle and hurt me. They should have known better than to use a morally offensive word against an innocent nine-year-old child. Ignorance is not bliss.

My view is that not all Jews were created equal. I believe this statement is correct when describing Soviet Jews. The USSR was a place that forbade the practice of one's religion while it encouraged generational hate. Strictly speaking, Soviet Jews, born in the USSR after the October Revolution in 1917, were not Jewish but, rather, Jews by default since they were not allowed to practise Judaism.

It started with a birth certificate which, once issued, predestined the fate of Jews. The infamous 'pyataya stroka' or 'fifth line' required the child's nationality. Commonly, elsewhere in the world, the place of birth predetermines a person's ethnicity, but not in the Soviet Union. The fact that my place of birth was Kazakhstan did not matter to the bureaucrats. My parents could not register me as a Kazakh. Mama obediently wrote Jewish as my nationality because my ancestors had practised Judaism for generations. My fate was sealed when the government assigned me a Jewish status and turned me into an object of discrimination. For 23 years, anti-Semitism followed me everywhere. It became my constant companion and my second shadow.

I experienced injustice on my first day of school when my first-grade teacher made fun of my name. I could not understand why she did it. She made me feel that I did not belong. As a result of this, my classmates took sides. Some supported me, while others supported the teacher. I was determined to learn and do my best, as I had promised my parents. Getting good grades was easy, but breaking the social barriers was hard. Every day, my classmates fought over me. I was not a fighter but my friends defended me. Almost once a week, we all went to the principal's office to hear yet another lecture on how certain things should not occur in a socialist society where everyone is equal.

My entire school life was like that. Then, on my graduation day in 1971, I received a red diploma, which is one of the highest academic honours. I was the second brightest student in my class. I should have had a gold medal, but my nationality denied me that. However, I felt lucky that the teachers had allowed me to receive such a distinguished prize. Standing in front of the podium, I felt proud and gave a speech. For me, it was a glorious opportunity to show my ill-wishers that they could not dampen my spirit. In that instance, I felt victorious. As I walked off the stage, I took a deep breath and thought that my struggles were finally over. I could go into the world to pursue my dream of a college education.

The red diploma gave me an advantage in taking the entrance exam. If I passed the composition with an 'A' grade, my admission would be guaranteed. Still naïve, I thought that anti-Semitism was local. I was great at writing and some of my stories had been published in the local newspaper, so I did not expect to get a lesser grade. I wrote an excellent piece, anticipating an 'A', but I got a 'B' and then had to take three more tests to be admitted.

I knew I would continue to face many battles.

The math-professor raised her eyebrows when she said my first name 'Etya' but, by the time she read my last name 'Vaserman', her eyes were about to pop out of their sockets. She put down my application and, without blinking an eye, asked me in a heavy Moldovan accent, "Tell me in Russian the formula of the quadratic equation." By then, I had had enough of her insinuations. I stared at her and, in perfect Russian, said, "I thought I was speaking to you in my native language already." I knew she did not like my answer. She bombarded me with questions that went outside the school curricula and, like a trooper, I answered them all. I was surprised when she gave me a 'B'. With that mark, and being Jewish, my chances of getting into college were slim but I was determined to try.

My next exam was in Physics, which I excelled at. The professor took time to gruel me and ask extra questions that were not on my test card. When he could not trick me into giving him the wrong answer, he said, "Young lady, you won't be accepted this year. I lower your score to 'C' but, if you come the following year, I will help you. Come and find me." It was obvious that he wanted a bribe. Devastated, I went back to my dorm room and cried myself to sleep. Seeing no point in staying for my last exam, I left the following morning.

Two years later, I was accepted onto a two-year college course without any entrance exams. The committee had no choice because I had graduated with a red diploma.

I met my future husband at college. Three months later, we married and, when our daughter turned two, we filled out immigration paperwork to move to the United States of America. I did not want the hate to win or my child to suffer. I wanted my daughter to grow up in a more positive world. Thankfully, in the late sixties, the Soviets lifted the Iron Curtain and the rest of the world found out about the mistreatment of the Soviet Jews. Our permission was granted based on religious discrimination and, on 7th March 1978, we took our first steps on 'the land of the free and the home of the brave'. Since then, I have never looked back or desired to visit the country that took away my identity. Moving to the USA meant that I tasted freedom for the first time in my life and it was the most incredible feeling in the world. I did not have to look over my shoulder as I walked the streets of New York. I felt like I belonged. Coming to my adopted country, I became enough. At last, I could be me.

Growing up in the Soviet Union, the only support I had was the love of my family. My parents cheered me up and stood by me when I felt low. They encouraged me to be better and not succumb to hate. Loyal friends also helped me to get through my ordeal. They loved me for who I was. When I came to the United States, I finally felt accepted, regardless of my origin.

When I look back at my life, I feel triumphant because I have never allowed myself to become a victim. I refused to let anti-Semitism take control of my life. For me, victimhood was never an option. My understanding of the injustice done to Jewish people made me determined to fight for what was right. Since that fateful day, when I discovered my identity from the woman who buried my innocence in a pile of snow, I knew I had to be strong. I was not a quitter.

In the end, my perseverance paid off. I have become a more insightful, kind and less judgmental person. The painful experiences I went through, growing up in USSR as a Jew, have helped me become stronger and more compassionate. Although prejudice is inherent in humanity, I genuinely wish for the cycle of hate to be eliminated. A bias of any kind should not prevail in civilised societies. I hope whoever reads this will understand intolerance better, as it comes in many forms, shapes and colours. My story is an example of how being different can cause a pivotal change. It certainly did for me. My experience taught me to become more responsible. I learned to adapt instead of falling apart in unfair situations. I became more educated, and I chose love over hate.

Like a beautiful butterfly, I came out of a cocoon, spread my wings and embraced life. Forgiveness brought me joy and taught me that I am enough.

Sarah's Reflections

Trigger your tenacity. Etya had to deal with prejudice as a child and this unfortunate 'state of lack' followed her into adulthood, but she did not give up. She had something to prove and wanted to ensure she would never allow others to dictate her choices. You can be at risk of losing your fighting spirit if things feel too hard, but with tenacity comes persistence. You must do whatever it takes to get what you want. How can you step-up and take action today?

Plant your own seeds. It is awful to be given a label that you feel you will never shake off. No one should ever have to suffer judgement; however, this spurred Etya on as she believed she deserved better. You may need to scatter many seeds, but when you decide to be your own cheerleader, you will reap the rewards. It is inevitable that some seeds will flourish.

Choose love. Love is a beautiful thing. You can hold on to bad feelings, have a grudge against someone who did you wrong many years ago, or have cross words with a close friend and not speak; but what purpose does it serve? Who does it help if you hold on to things from the past and keep damaging emotions deep inside? You must channel that negative energy into a more positive place, and be relentless in your pursuit of happiness, just as Etya did when she moved to Florida.

10
Richard Thomas

'If you don't ask you don't get' – Gareth Thomas

I was bullied at work.
I used to find it extremely difficult to talk about.

It started in 1998 when I was in my 40s, chasing ambition and promotion. I had spent more than 20 years working in the Civil Service and had matured as a successful junior manager, keen to progress. I have always been accustomed to open and collaborative communication. My new role was developing novel legislation, which was completely out of my comfort zone, but I was happy that I had the skills and experience to do the job well. I was also flattered that the interview board considered me suitable for the role.

I quickly found myself in a downward spiral working with a small team of colleagues who were scared to say anything. Even in one-to-one conversations, they were reluctant to share their views or think beyond daily tasks. Our boss was an ambitious senior leader who only had one way to manage; through fear, oppression and unrealistic demands. I had been warned by a colleague when I started and I remember thinking, 'That can't be right.' My colleagues were unwilling to challenge her and, no matter how I tried, she seemed unable to draw on my experiences or delegate tasks. Instead, she adopted a dictatorial approach which undermined and challenged my values.

At the time, I had not associated my emotions and self-doubt with bullying, which was created by the organisational culture. It was only on reflection, many months after the event, that I made the connection. My initial thoughts were that it was my fault; I felt incapable, totally isolated and devalued. Some of my experiences did not help to deliver a rounded, coordinated programme and I believed that my senior manager's behaviour was down to her fear of being inadequate and unable to deliver. There were many situations where I was made to feel uncomfortable. I was instructed not to discuss planning requirements outside the immediate team. My conflict here was that I needed others to support the project, help with resources and manage the legal requirements. It was obvious that my manager did not trust others and felt that asking outside her team would expose her weaknesses and failures.

I had unrealistic demands made of me, where ministerial briefing papers were requested at short notice, only to be told a day later 'not to bother' as my manager had done them. Teamwork was not in her vocabulary. There was no discussion or consultation. Work was uncoordinated and erratic, with plans having to be finished at short notice despite delivery dates known in advance. Lack of trust in anything I, or anyone else, did seemed to be the norm with subtle threatening and coercive language used to belittle us. My style of openness and engagement was 'not the way we do it here'. I dreaded going to work. On reflection, the worst part was that my boss did not trust me, did not value my skillset and did not treat me as a human being. It was the worst experience of my life.

The situation came to a head on a family holiday in Orlando, Florida. The lightbulb moment came when we were in SeaWorld and the kids were encouraging me to join them at the dolphin petting pool just as the centre was closing. I suddenly realised that there was nothing more important than that time with the kids, especially when a dolphin swam under my hand as it lay on the pool's surface. It was a life-changing moment.

However, when we got home, I had worked myself into a state and was unable to face going back to work. I had thought through what I wanted to say to my boss, but I felt physically sick thinking about the conversation. The effort on my first day going back to work was tremendous. I stopped many times on the way there, wondering if I could see it through but I resolved to keep going as I had to break the cycle.

When I arrived at work, my boss was off sick. I had so much tension, anger and self-doubt built up inside at that point, I had to confront someone. I decided to go and see my manager's boss who, in terms of civil service leadership, was a senior director reporting directly to the department's minister. I wanted to dump my anger right at the top. I was barely able to contain myself, but I insisted that he listen to me. I explained what had been happening, shared my feelings and told him that I would be leaving, as I could no longer work under such oppressive conditions. Even at that point, I had not twigged that I was a victim of bullying. I finished what I needed to say, gave him no opportunity to respond and left the building.

When I got home, I told my wife what had happened. She listened calmly, giving unconditional emotional support, and helped me expose my fears and concerns. My thoughts were all over the place and, over the following few days, I ruminated on the consequences of my actions but remained resolved not to return to work. I agreed to see my GP, who signed me off work due to emotional distress. I have a logical approach to most things so, when I started to plan my next steps, I began to consider the worst thing that could happen. This next bit will sound weird, but I thought about how I would feel if my teenage daughter got pregnant. Although it would be life-changing, I decided that I could live with that so, on balance, I did not feel as overwhelmed with my decision.

After a short time, I was invited by HR to consider counselling by way of rehabilitation, which I was happy to do. I had never experienced counselling first-hand before, so I had no framework in which to measure my expectations. I saw it initially as the route to return to my former employer. I was nervous and apprehensive as the first meeting was in the building where I had worked. Fear of meeting up with my line manager was overwhelming, but the counsellor was exceptionally supportive. I had already formulated a plan on what I wanted to achieve, which was my way of controlling the situation, and I had already contacted my former HR team to initiate things.

Counselling took several months, and the sessions allowed me to express my thoughts, albeit incoherently at first. Subsequent sessions were less traumatic. We worked through my issues of how the bullying had manifested itself and why I felt unable to return to that working environment. The sessions taught me two things.

The first was a technique to expel my negative thoughts. I wrote a letter to my line manager and included all my emotions. I recall sitting in the garden one afternoon, doing this. It was a cathartic moment to free my mind of the mental negativity. I still have the letter, and I have since suggested the technique to others who have experienced their own challenges.

The second thing I learned was alarming and angered me more. My line manager had a history of bullying and I was the sixth person in that role since the previous five managers had all left under similar circumstances. I refocussed my anger on the organisation, which had arguably been aware of, and condoned, the pattern of endemic behaviour and chose to do nothing.

With help from the counsellor, I was able to make arrangements to return to my previous department. I had to relinquish my promotion but I was content to do so. Returning felt like a homely comfort blanket, but resentment did stay with me for a while.

As I regained confidence, my self-belief returned and I started to realise that it was not my fault. That helped me on an upward spiral of well-being, and I finally felt supported by being back in an open organisation. Workwise, I felt valued as I was again trusted and allowed to act independently with delegated responsibilities. I became confident in my achievements, was more open about my emotions and recognised my stress signs and those of others around me. I was more relaxed at home; still task-oriented, but happier and content, having decided that we were still financially stable.

My counsellor's suggestion to write down all my concerns and emotions was a pivotal moment. Some were harsh realities of life but, even they, were learning points. From the moment I 'snapped' to when I recovered some composure and self-belief was less than a couple of months. I believe I was able to regain control because of my wife and counsellor's support and my own personal drive to 'get back onto an even keel'. Planning and organising are my strengths and once I had decided that I had wallowed long enough, it was time to refocus, realising it was possible to return to my previous employer as a route to recovery.

I wrote to the senior director and HR department, to seek closure and express my views on their organisation's prevailing secretive and mistrusting environment. I took a more sanguine approach to work. It felt like it was less about seeking advancement and more about being the best person I could be. I was happy with the new me and my approach to work was different. Surprisingly, since that experience, my ambition has changed but most unexpectedly, and without trying, my career flourished exponentially. I never did get a response, but it felt good to air my views.

Why have I chosen to write about this and share it now?

Because it does not hurt anymore. I have used my experience, and what I have learnt, to influence others positively and, if I can reach a wider audience, that is all the better. Bullying is a horrible experience to have to deal with. It took me to a dark and uncomfortable place. The key message I want to get across is that people often internalise what is happening. Our emotions and experiences shape our thoughts, and sometimes we think that things are our fault or that we are not good enough. You may need help to appreciate that, as I did, through a counsellor who helped me reassess and reassert my values. If you feel this way, ask for help. Talk to someone. It is so important. When sharing, you might have to face up to some realities, but talking is a great way to do this and work through the pain so that you can move forward.

I was able to share it with my staff before I retired and, more recently, with family and friends. Now, years later, it is hard to put this into context but, at the time, it was scary and challenged my beliefs; but my aim was always to regain control of my life. I wanted to make sure that I could support my family, pay the bills and be happy.

Now my children are grown up and I have grandchildren. I am financially sound in retirement and, most importantly, I am happy.

Sarah's Reflections

Your moral compass. You have things that light you up, which have been shaped by your family, culture, religion, education and personal experiences. Your values and beliefs reflect your moral compass and are the main driving force around how you view life and your choices. These can evolve and change many times in your lifetime. As Richard understood his values, he knew when his boundaries had been crossed.

Identifying your values is a great exercise. Write a list of 20 words that describe your values – some examples are security, family, adventure, connection and money. Then prioritise 5-10 which resonate with you the most. To go deeper, you can write a brief explanation of each, describing why it is important and how it influences your decisions and actions. Reflect and compare your current life with these values. You may notice a mismatch, where you think you are not meeting some of your values, so adjustments are needed to make you happier.

Courage creates change. Richard quickly realised that he was not comfortable in his new role. He did not know what to do or where to turn. It is difficult when you feel lost and stuck. Anxiety builds and it can become a rollercoaster ride of pessimistic mind talk. You must always believe you are important and that your feelings matter. Do not sit in silence. Richard knew he had to break the cycle. It took a lot of courage, but his first reaction was to protect himself. After support from his

GP and counsellor, he was able to see more clearly and take action.

Writing heals. Putting your private thoughts onto paper can provide a well-needed sanctuary. Holding pain inside can damage your psyche and cause many problems. Allowing yourself to let go is liberating. I often journal which brings relief to thoughts stuck in my head and, as the words tumble out, the pressure eases. Richard wrote a letter that he never shared, but it released a lot of pent-up tension and allowed him to find closure. This was an important part of his healing journey.

11
Des Reynolds

'The greatest glory in living lies not in falling, but in rising every time we fall' – Nelson Mandela

It has been over 10 years since we lost our daughter, Ruby, just six hours after she was born.

I have seen a lot written about the impact that losing a baby has on a mother but, extraordinarily, I have found little about the impact on the father. My aim in writing this is to convey how it felt from my point of view, how it has impacted my life since and to hopefully encourage other men who have suffered a loss to open up about their feelings.

We had been nervous throughout the pregnancy as we felt there may not be many more chances, given our age.

Everything had been going ok until Ruby was born, unexpectedly and prematurely, before 23 weeks. At that level of prematurity, survival is possible but unlikely. She did survive for several hours which spanned two calendar days and, initially, there were promising signs and talk of a transfer to another hospital. I even went to my nearby flat to have a shower and get changed in preparation for the move. But when three doctors came in, with grave looks on their faces, we knew what they were going to say.

The first time we got to hold our baby daughter was as the nurses were turning off the machines that were keeping her alive. My automatic response was to support my partner (now my wife). All I wanted was to help take the pain away as, instinctively, I believed that it would be worse for her than for me. In reality, my entire world had just fallen apart. We then had to sit in a room with our dead child (even writing about that now is incredibly difficult). No matter how painful those last moments were; looking back, I realise how vital they were. I treasure that half-hour, almost as much as the six hours she was alive, because she was still with us. I could look at her face and know she existed. There were still the three of us. I did not want her to go. We took photos but, frustratingly, the flash did not work and most were too dark. We did get some pictures of us together and they provide precious memories.

I could not comprehend how life still went on around us. I know this may be cliché, but how could other people get on with their lives when this had happened to us? People we knew were going about their lives as normal, so how do you tell them what has happened? Text, phone? What is the etiquette for this? I had no clue how to tell people.

I sent a generic text to close friends which must have been as horrible to receive as it was to write. I did not feel I could tell my parents over the phone, so I went to see them. It was the worst taxi ride ever, even though it was only a mile away. My parents, and several other family members, came to see her. They will never know how much this meant to us. Everyone who saw Ruby validated her in some way.

Then comes the journey home from the hospital, without your baby. You arrive back to a house that you have been preparing, ready for the new arrival. Our home felt empty and almost without hope. We had to remove the obvious signs. In our case, it never felt like the right place to be after we lost Ruby, so we moved a few years later.

The next couple of weeks went by in a blur. We had my stepson to look after. He probably will not appreciate how much this helped us, and I grew closer to him during that time. We have never taken for granted that we had other children, which now includes our son Jack, who came along just when we thought any chance had almost gone. People might think that having other children makes losing a child easier, but it does not lessen the loss. Somebody remarked to us, "You have another child though?" Yes, we did, but we should have had two, and then three. However, what it does do is give you something positive to focus on, with familiar routines and the incentive to try to make their lives wonderful.

We then had to plan our daughter's funeral. I am still proud of the music we chose, *Ruby*, *Greatest Day* and *One More Angel in Heaven*. It is amazing how these songs appear in our lives, even now. I managed to carry her coffin and even make a speech. It was one of the last things I was able to do for her.

I am grateful to every single person who came to the funeral. It was not an easy place to be, but it helped us immensely, knowing we had support.

Then you go home and are expected to get on with your life. Or, in my case, you almost fall apart the next day when all the emotions come out. I was watching a show about the snooker player, Alex Higgins, who had just died and there was a famous clip where his baby daughter was placed in his arms after a world title. I was in total bits as I knew I would never get to experience a moment like that with Ruby. I have never cried like that before, or since. I know I needed to because something was taken out of my system and, in the long term, it undoubtedly helped, rather than having all that pent-up emotion hiding inside me.

One thing that did not help me was my work. I had recently changed jobs and had only been in the company a few months. I did not know anyone well and had not had the chance to build up a good reputation. I took a maximum of two weeks of sick leave and returned to reduced hours, at my suggestion. Unfortunately, it was horrible. I can appreciate that it was difficult for them, but most people had no idea what to say, so said nothing. A few colleagues were outstandingly supportive, including the company's nurse but, alarmingly, one colleague told me that I should 'get over it'. That is one of the worst things you can say to someone who has just lost a child because you will never 'get over' losing a baby. My probationary period was extended because they had not seen 'the best of me' which, in my opinion, was hardly surprising in the circumstances. I got a letter from my doctor to try to explain why I lacked 'spark', but it was too late. My contract was terminated a few months later. Losing my job, on top of losing my daughter, was awful. That was the first time that I had ever been dismissed from a role and it came as a blow to my confidence when I was already at an all-time low.

Fortunately, an old boss provided temporary employment which kept me going and enabled me to do a project to finish my MBA. This gave me something positive to focus on which, I believe, is vital for someone bereaved. I have continued working in manufacturing for most of my career but have found it difficult to trust bosses since, and I certainly lost any ambition to climb the career ladder. I did try some counselling for a short while; however, it became an opportunity to moan about work and did not help me with feelings about bereavement.

So how can you find positives going through something like this? In my case, it accelerated over time with a desire to do something positive, in memory of Ruby, as a way of keeping her name alive. I contacted Lucy Herd, having listened to her being interviewed on Radio 5 one evening. She was fundraising for the charity *Jack's Rainbow*, and this seemed an obvious project to get involved with. They were looking to buy a caravan as a place where families, who had lost children, could go for a funded holiday. I decided to set myself a series of challenges to help them raise funds. The first project was a sponsored ten-pin bowling event, setting myself a target of scoring 2015 pins in 15 games. People could sponsor me and guess a 'nearest the pin' total. I ran a team competition on the same night and, although I missed my pin target, I did manage to raise over £2k.

I liked the idea of trying for a Guinness World Record, which culminated in an attempt to set the record for the largest ever Sports Quiz in January 2017. A fantastic team of friends helped me organise the quiz and we managed to get some sporting celebrities, such as Nick Skelton, Phil Tufnell and Dion Dublin to record video questions. We also got some fantastic prizes for both the auction and raffle. Unfortunately, we fell a few short of Guinness' target with 420 people so there was no official record, although I still legitimately claim an unofficial world record! More importantly, over £7k was raised which was split between *Jack's Rainbow* and *Myton Hospice* in Warwick.

I still have ambitions to raise enough to fund the caravan for *Jack's Rainbow* and also have another attempt at the world record. COVID delayed any more events, but I plan to start thinking of some new ideas to raise money in the coming years. I have gained so much from running community fundraisers. Firstly, I have seen how positive friends and family can be in supporting me with the challenges. Secondly, having a project to focus on, in aid of a cause you believe in, can motivate you like nothing else. I seek out opportunities to make a positive difference in others' lives, such as volunteering for charities, coaching children to play cricket and being a trustee for a local nursery. These have ultimately led to me now working in a local special educational needs school where I find my contribution is making a difference to children, in some way, which makes me very happy.

Nobody should have to see their child die before them. It is contrary to the natural order of things. It rips your whole world apart. The one thing a parent is supposed to do, before anything else, is to protect their children. Nothing can ever take away the feeling that you could not stop your child from dying. Nothing can ever bring our baby back.

My advice, for anyone going through something similar, is to be kind to yourself and those around you. It is ok not to be ok. You may find support from some unexpected people. Try not to be too hard on friends who do not offer support, as it will be difficult for them too. Things will get easier over time, although they will never be as they were. Hopefully, like me, you can find some meaning to your life that will surprise you, or even experience post-traumatic growth where you manage to find personal growth after traumatic events. I would never have done any charity events if we had not lost Ruby. I treasure time with my other children and appreciate the opportunity to be part of their lives even more.

I want to encourage men to talk about their feelings more and to reach out to others to support them to do this. There should be no expectation for them to 'man up' and not show their emotions. If you try to hold things in, it will catch up with you in the end. All sorts of organisations can help with this. Please do not suffer in silence.

I am so proud of how our daughter battled for her life.

I still grieve for her and the potential of all she could have been. An important benefit is knowing that I am able to keep Ruby's name alive so that her brief life still has a positive impact on many other people. I thank her for that. She will always be part of our family.

In memory of our daughter, Ruby Elizabeth Mary Reynolds.

Sarah's Reflections

You are not alone. No matter how you feel, there will always be someone who can offer support. You may want to hide from the world but you eventually realise you need to resurface. People are kind and will want to help. There are no set rules to who, how and when. The first step is to reach out. Having someone to talk to is vital. You may read this and want your life to remain private. Not everyone likes to share their deepest thoughts and feelings, however all 21 people within this book found comfort when they opened up to others.

Bouncebackability. Des introduced me to this phrase. An ability to bounce back when you have experienced loss. It reflects the 'growing around grief' model by Lois Tonkin, which acknowledges that the grief will never go away, but the person grows around it. There are definite processes and emotional waves to find your own suitable coping mechanisms. Dr Victoria Wilson-Crane wrote an amazing book on dealing with grief, called *Sixteen Days.*

It is ok not to be ok. There may be an expectation of making sure you are in a positive space and staying upbeat, but you must give yourself permission to have an off day or even an off week. When you are faced with trauma, there will be endless days when you feel awful and, as the months go by, you might set yourself an expectation that you should be 'over it by now'. Why should you? You wake up, emotions are high, everything feels raw and you are back in the moment, where your grief and loss are unbearable. Give yourself all the time you need.

12
Chris Duncan

'Breathe. You are alive!' – Thich Nhat Hanh

To anyone else, discovering that they were seriously ill would be devastating. To me, it was liberating.

Over 17 years of declining health, the 'quiet killer' had slowly been sucking the life out of me. My diagnosis went unrealised as my body and mind gradually shut down.

My tiny stature was attributed to my mother's lack of height. Oozing rashes were discounted as eczema. Fatigue and weakness were directed at my unwillingness to work. Dark circles under my eyes were assumed to be caused by a lack of sleep. I never told anyone that I would forget the directions from home to high school every day, or when my knees hurt with every step I took. I did not even complain about the onset of my urinary tract infections or kidney infections because I thought the pain was normal. I thought, if I said anything, I would be labelled a hypochondriac like my beloved grandmother, whom some regarded with disdain.

At the age of 17, I could not walk laps due to the terrible aches in my knees. My back began to hurt too, but I chalked it up to carting around too many textbooks. I had waited until the last possible moment to take the required gym class. My senior year had arrived, and my teacher did not want any excuses. She looked at my 78lbs frame and declared that I would fail if I did not participate. The thought of not being able to graduate horrified me, as fears of being 'less than' or 'not enough' were constantly in my head. A doctor's note was my last resort to get out of the class, but I knew that my mom did not have the money for one. It caused me great turmoil to insist upon it and we scheduled a trip to the doctor for the following week.

That gym teacher was the catalyst in saving my life.

The next morning, I could barely drive myself to school due to the pain. Parking my brown Chevette in front of the school, I rested my head on the steering wheel, willing my back to stop hurting. Gritting my teeth, I lugged the stack of books and my diminutive frame up the sidewalk, into school. My classroom was still locked, so I slunk down on the floor. Without warning, vomit filled my throat. As quickly as I could, I picked myself up off the floor and headed to the restroom. I did not make it in time. The wretchedness filling my throat spewed towards the long dark hair of a girl who was walking in front of me. I ran into the bathroom, not waiting to see the girl's response and emptied what was left in my stomach.

The school bell rang for the first period. I left the toilet, retrieved my books from the floor by the classroom door and headed to the school office to request permission to go home. "You can only go home if you throw up," she said, blandly. "I threw up everywhere," I stammered weakly, wondering if she would believe me and let me leave. I thankfully had the strength to drive myself home. I took myself to bed and waited for my mom to come back home from work. I explained what had happened and she booked me an appointment immediately.

The following week, the doctors insisted that, "she looks fine to me," dismissing my slight frame, oozing rash and gigantic circles around my eyes. My mom insisted that they did something. Finally, they agreed to do a blood test. We were told that the results would take a few hours, so my dad took me to an orthodontist appointment while my mom waited. I had only just walked in the door to the clinic when the lab called and told them not to touch me as I should return straightaway. They acted as though they were scared of me. We left, smirking at the ridiculousness of it all, with no clue as to what was about to happen next.

When we arrived back, my mom and dad were ushered into a room with me. Two doctors and a nurse entered and soberly told me that I needed a bone marrow transplant and described the method in painful detail. They disappeared and we were silent. I was left teary-eyed and shell-shocked.

Two minutes later, another nurse came in and asked rapid-fire questions. I was mortified with such personal questions.

"How often do you urinate?" "What colour is it?" "Does it hurt when you urinate?" On and on they interrogated me, frustrated that I had no answers. Reality had become surreal. Two more doctors rushed into the room.

"Do you realise you would have died in less than two weeks if you hadn't come in today? You are in kidney failure, and we need to start dialysis right away."

Blank stares resulted in a brief explanation. It had not been eczema plaguing me, as they had assured us since infancy. Instead, toxins were being forced through my skin as my kidneys were unable to do their job. I was relieved. This sounded better than a bone marrow transplant. And, even better, I was not a hypochondriac after all. There were reasons for my perceived flaws. I remember thinking, maybe I was 'enough'.

A nephrologist came to see us, and her gentle Indian accent relaxed me. The plan was to put a catheter into my neck and utilise a machine to do the work for my kidneys. She explained that a shot near my collarbone would numb the forthcoming pain to stabilise me. While she spoke, I focused on the diamond ring in her nose. I felt the catheter tube push through my skin and my heart seemed to vibrate. I was frantic and struggled to breathe but her kind face looked in my eyes as she soothed me with her gentle voice, asking me to breathe deeply.

It took time for me to get out of that critical condition. A wonderful woman called Mary Hansen came to our home for a while and taught me how to use a home-based dialysis machine, with a tube through my stomach instead of my neck. It meant that I did not have to go to the clinic for hours every day. She was so kind and patient, full of vitality and such a support for keeping me positive and helping me to foster an 'I can do it' attitude. I was thrilled to be feeling better. A teacher from my high school came to my home every day to ensure that I could finish the school program and graduate.

My dad was amazing during that time. If anyone ever deserved an award for 'Super Carer', it would be him. He learned about cleanliness and safety and was an avid listener as they taught us how to clamp one tube to another to prevent peritonitis, which can be deadly. So, at night, with my dad's help, I hooked myself up to my machine. We had to ensure that vents were closed, tubes were clamped, masks were on and hands were washed as if my life depended on it. Because it did. In between taking care of me, my dad worked. As I started to stabilise, a kidney transplant became a good option. Dad offered me the greatest gift. Five months later, we went into surgery together and he donated a kidney to me.

"*#@!#@!*" I awoke to hear myself cursing, something I had never done in my entire life. Unspeakable pain seared my abdomen as I was lifted from the bedsheets onto a cold metal slab before being returned to the bed. My cousin Esther sat by the window and smiled at me. I had just enough time to be mortified at my behaviour before I drifted back into oblivion. Eight days later, I walked into the most inviting place in the world - home.

Organ donation is most certainly a gift of life.

I have achieved so much since then. I was able to walk up the aisle for my high school graduation and go to the senior prom. Those were my first moments back in the world and I was just so happy to finally be living. I ended up going to college and getting a bachelor's degree. I did a summer study program in France, the place I had dreamt of. I even had a group of friends for the first time in my life. I got married and had a child, which was the one unshakable 'want' in my life.

My son is the absolute joy of my life. Having a child was hard on my transplant and already-failing kidney (that had lasted me 14 years), but being a mom is the most amazing and fulfilling experience. Every day, I watch my son grow, learn and evolve. He is full of humour and compassion, as well as obstinance and, at times, unregulated emotions. As I raise him, I grow and evolve too. His father and I unfortunately parted ways after 18 years together.

My mom has always been my constant, a stalwart figure in my life and, without her and my father, I would not be where I am today. Their support, along with my extended family, the school system, the nursing staff and the doctors helped keep me uplifted. It would have been so easy to sink to rock bottom without them. Uncle Rokus and Aunt Carolynne inspired my self-will into action. They often spoke about following one's heart and it is through this that my healing journey continues. I now trust my instincts when something in my body feels 'off'. I no longer bow to doctors insisting that everything seems normal when I know it is not. I trust the skills and knowledge of doctors, but I trust my experience and my body enough to question them or, at least, to insist on more lab work.

When I was 21, just four years after my first kidney transplant, the doctors told me that there was nothing more they could do. As you can imagine, that was shocking news. I am a fighter and did not want to give up, but I felt helpless and did not know what to do. I turned to God to help me and felt a strong connection with a scripture from the Bible. Acts 17:28 "For in Him, we live and move and have our being." God helped me through for many years. I have had three kidney transplants and have struggled with bouts of anger and upset, but now I can accept who I need to be. I still have faith in something, but I am a little unsure what that looks like. More recently, I have felt strongly drawn to nature for the healing of my soul.

My friend, and health geek, Nelson works as my dietary endocrinologist. He enables me to persevere with the aid of naturopathic help by providing combinations of food and vitamin supplements and changing them when necessary. Working as a team, with him and my doctors, yields better results. Listening to others is also helpful so that I can combine their knowledge with my experience.

If I could talk to my younger self, or anyone experiencing unexplainable symptoms, I would say this, "Listen to your body. Trust your instincts. Do not be afraid to tell your parents or guardians." The repercussions of not listening to my body and keeping it to myself were huge. I was so concerned about being seen as 'less than' or 'not enough' that I bowed to others' opinions and nearly died because of it. Be bold and discuss your symptoms so that you know what is normal and what needs attention. Even with a chronic illness, you can still live a fulfilling life.

My life was allowed to go on, thanks to organ donation. I will be forever grateful to my donors. Physically, I am healthy and mostly stable. Cognitively, I am better now as I do not have to deal with constant brain fog. I have learned so much over the years and feel fulfilled as I have grown. My anxiety has reduced, I have gained a better perspective and I can enjoy many moments. Life is precious and I intend to make the most of the rest of my days.

I hope you will deliberately enjoy each day too, as if it is the final full day of your extraordinary, ordinary life.

Sarah's Reflections

Fight your corner. 'Be bold' is a strong message from Chris. As humans we do not like to cause a fuss or draw attention to ourselves. We often avoid situations in case we get the news we do not want to hear. The 'put your head in the sand and then it's not real' scenarios. It takes courage and confidence to speak up. You must find your voice so that you are heard.

Feel-good factor. Chris realised that taking care of her health was critical. Nutrition and fitness go hand-in-hand when looking after your well-being. When you are at your lowest, meals may be skipped or you reach for bad food as an easy choice. You must nourish and fuel your body to make you stronger. How much water do you drink? Why not try adding lemons or a sprinkle of cinnamon to make it tastier? Exercise is sometimes low on our list of priorities, but if you make it more of a necessity then the happy endorphins are guaranteed to give you a boost. Research shows that exercising 2-3 times a week can help with symptoms of depression.

Eyes wide open. Chris is alive, thanks to several organ donors. When faced with uncertainty, it makes you pause and reflect, which can give you the clarity you need to notice what is special in your life. When going through the mundane routine of eat, sleep, work and repeat, you can take things for granted. You need to open your eyes to notice precious moments in everyday living. What would help you open your eyes wider?

13
Tanith Lee

'God, grant me the serenity to accept the things I cannot change, courage to change the things I can, and wisdom to know the difference' – The Serenity Prayer

I knew I had a problem with booze. A big problem. From the first time I started drinking and taking drugs, at the age of 14, I did it addictively and always wanted more.

I experienced bullying in my teens which came in the form of name-calling. I was ginger, lanky and had terrible acne, so I was an easy target and they would often wait for me after school. My most horrible memory was when I had a few friends around and the bullies appeared and took over my house. I was stuck in my bedroom, terrified. Downstairs, they were running riot, drinking my mum's alcohol and destroying the carpet with cigarette burns. The next day, I told my mum what had happened and she said that her rings were missing. I had to tell the police and we found out that they had sold the rings for money to buy drugs.

I had some great times with my 'friend' booze, but then it stopped being my friend. I knew, deep down, that I had a problem but did not want to face it. I would get defensive if anyone questioned how much I was drinking and using. I remember my mum having the audacity to suggest that I was depressed because I was drinking too much. How right she was.

As I grew older, I had ongoing periods of depression. I was starting to experience blackouts, when I could not remember the night before, and my moral compass was most definitely broken. When under the influence, I behaved in ways that brought me shame and guilt and the only way I knew how to deal with those emotions was to drink even more. My mental health declined significantly and, at the age of 19, I took an overdose.

In my early twenties, I half-heartedly tried ways to feel better with exercise and yoga. They helped, for a while, but did not get to the root of the problem. I was arrogant and aggressive at that age but it was because I was scared and my solution was to build a wall around myself. I had periods of not drinking but it was very difficult and deeply uncomfortable, so they did not last long. I got married when I was 27 and had my first child at 29. When I was pregnant, I did manage to cut back on drinking, but I am ashamed to say that I did not have the willpower to stop it completely.

In 2004, I moved from South London to West Sussex. My husband worked long hours in London and I was alone with young children to look after. Again, I found myself turning to my old 'friend' as a coping mechanism. I lived in mental hell for five years but I was still managing to function on the outside. Most of the time, I hid it well but occasionally I would go out and get spectacularly drunk and high and embarrass myself and others.

I knew I was beginning to unravel inside. I was depressed, anxious, paranoid and felt broken and unfixable. I reached out to my GP for help and was referred to an alcohol and drugs counsellor who did her best but, like a typical addict, I lied about how much I was drinking and using. I lied about so much back then. I did not know how to be honest. I wanted someone to fix me and teach me how to drink moderately, as 'normal' people did.

The counsellor suggested that I go to 12-Step meetings. The word 'abstinence' terrified me. Give up drinking? How on earth would I live without booze? It was unimaginable. I felt desperate, so I made a call to the helpline to attend a recovery meeting, but I cancelled at the last minute. I carried on drinking for another year, finally hitting rock bottom. I knew, if I did not act, I would lose everything. It felt like a life-or-death decision. I know that sounds dramatic but that is where the addiction took me. I contacted the recovery helpline and they arranged for me to attend another meeting.

2nd January 2009 marked the beginning of my sobriety journey. Walking into that room was one of the scariest things I have ever done in my life. My heart was pounding and every cell in my body told me to run away. The addictive voice was saying, "You're not that bad." I am glad I ignored that voice. I needed help!

I sat down and stared at my feet, feeling confused, scared, lost and alone. People started sharing their stories and thoughts of shame, guilt, despair and self-disgust that I recognised so well but had kept hidden away deep inside for years. I also listened with interest to their stories of freedom. At the end of the meeting, people reassured me that I could get better and that there was hope. That emotion felt alien to me, but I had sensed something magical in the room. On the drive home, I felt elated and finally there was an ember of hope, warm in my heart. I finally felt like I belonged somewhere.

That was the beginning of a new chapter.

Since that day, I have not had a drop of alcohol or touched drugs, but it was not easy. I had terrible cravings and was riding on the world's biggest emotional roller coaster. Living as 'Tanith', without my crutch, was awful. I went through tears, anger, fear and apathy in a seemingly endless loop. I had picked up my first drug, aged only 14, and now I felt like that terrified teenager all over again but, this time, with no way to release my feelings.

I discovered that sobriety is much more than giving up alcohol and drugs. It is also about learning how to become aware of my feelings, emotions and thoughts. Drinking and using were the result of my emotional state and mental well-being.

The 12-Steps showed me how unmanageable my life had become, and how to:

- admit that I needed help with my addictions
- go back through my past and own my part in it
- find and connect to a power greater than myself
- make amends to those I had hurt
- continue to keep looking inward to ensure that I am a good human being
- learn self-reflection and meditation

I threw myself into recovery and my 'inner me' changed. I was happier, healthier and more content with being me. To the outside world, I probably looked like the same person but, on the inside, I was transforming. Slowly, I learned how to live without any substances. I had to do a lot of 'inner work' and face the shadows within me. It was tough but I was finally getting to the root cause of my addiction.

I realise now that this is a lifelong job, but I would not have it any other way. I know myself better. I have learned how to share what is really going on for me and I live a more spiritual life. Nature is my non-religious god and walking the dog in the beautiful countryside is my church. I do my best to live my life with kindness, tolerance and patience but I still get it wrong and make mistakes. When I meditate regularly, I feel amazing as the breathing and quietness make me content, calm and happy. To me, spirituality is an awareness; a feeling of warmth in my soul where there used to be blackness.

People often get confused and ask why, after 15 years of sobriety, I need to continue to go to recovery meetings. The easiest way to explain it is that I am surrounded by a loving, supportive community of like-minded people who have been with me on my journey since day one. They have seen me grow, as I have them. It provides connection, unconditional love, non-judgmental support and, most of all, joy and lots and lots of laughter. It is also our way of giving back; to be there for the newcomers who come in as scared, fearful, dazed and confused as I was. I have learned to share my vulnerability openly and help others on the same path. My marriage survived and I have an incredible bond with my children. I cannot imagine what those relationships would have been like if I had carried on with my old ways.

In my first year of sobriety, I also had a challenging diagnosis. I thought that the severe night sweats, in my 30s, were down to drinking but it turned out that they were due to early menopause. I remember the call from my doctor. I was in complete shock. I was aged 37, newly sober and now had the most insane hormonal ups and downs. The early menopause affected me psychologically more than physically. I went to some dark places and, at times, felt that I could not carry on living. After many doctors' appointments and seeing specialists, I was put on HRT and it was like someone had flipped the light switch back on. I felt like me again.

At that point, not many people were talking about menopause, as it was considered taboo. I decided to share my journey by blogging at www.mrsmenopause.co.uk and posting on social media. Women wanted to know more so I started running courses, workshops and talks. It gave me so much fulfilment to be able to help other women. In 2014, I enrolled on a three-year course to become a nutritional therapist. It was difficult going back to school as I had not done that well the first time round. When I finally got the email to say that I had passed, I was delighted with my achievement although, by that point, I knew that I was close to burnout.

Recently, something has shifted for me again. The COVID pandemic was a perfect time for me to step back and look at what I wanted to do next. Being 14-years post-menopause and sober, I have grown so much. I am now able to embrace the older, and much wiser, version of myself. I want to have deeper conversations and connections with women and get to the root cause of their midlife ups and downs. I really embrace the spiritual side of life, something I would have mocked in my arrogant younger years. I see so much joy and wonder in the world and am grateful every morning to be alive. In my darkest days, I used to be disappointed that I had woken up, let alone be grateful.

I love learning about how our minds work and am fascinated with the brain. I have been exploring my limiting self-beliefs which have held on tightly since my childhood. With the help of a mentor, who has taught me a brilliant mindset framework, I have been able to cut the ties to those old beliefs and start creating new ones. It has impacted my life so dramatically that I am training to coach others in the same method. I now know that all I ever wanted was freedom from the negative self-talk and inner critic, to feel safe and to love myself; I just did not know how to. I spent many years with an emptiness inside, feeling that I was broken and did not belong.

Writing all this reminds me of the journey I have been on, especially since putting down the booze and drugs. I am proud of the work I have done. No one could have done this for me. I had to grow up and take responsibility for myself. I lived in victim mode for so long, I felt the world was against me but now I know that the universe works with me when I let it.

Sometimes I feel like I am still a novice at life but that is a good thing. I hope I am always willing to learn and grow. As the saying goes, "Fall seven times, stand up eight."

Sarah's Reflections

EnCOURAGE. Are there things you want to do but a gremlin on your shoulder tells you, 'You won't be able to do it' or 'You'll make yourself look stupid'? The list is endless of ways you can talk yourself out of anything. Tanith knew she needed help but, each time, something stopped her, until she reached a turning point. A motivational book that helped me encourage my own courage to overcome a major challenge was, *Feel the Fear and Do it Anyway* by Susan Jeffers.

Finding your tribe. When you are struggling, you may not want to turn to your nearest and dearest. You either feel embarrassed sharing your thoughts or think they will not understand. Tanith describes how finding a sense of belonging was her pivotal moment. She made the decision to attend the 12-Step meeting and found her tribe there.

Be proud of who you are today. Life can often be frantic, so you may never pause and acknowledge what you have been through to get here. It is a wonderful feeling to stop and take time to write down key achievements and challenges you have overcome. Allowing yourself some quiet space is important. Why not book some time in your diary to be alone once a month; for an hour, or even half-a-day? Celebrate how awesome you are.

14

Carly Michael

'Just keep swimming' – Dory

I had been having a civilised 'school night' drink at a friend's house with a few of my mum mates. I left early and, as I pulled up to our house, the Bluetooth in my car connected to my husband's phone. The line was bad and the fuzz of my additional connection had changed the tone of the phone conversation. I heard a woman's voice asking if everything was ok. I kept quiet so as not to disturb the call and parked in silence. I assumed it was just a work colleague.

I walked into the house to see him sitting on the sofa. I asked who he was talking to, and he replied, "Nobody… I wasn't on the phone." When I explained the Bluetooth in the car, he backtracked and said it was a male friend. I knew it was a woman's voice, so I questioned him but he remained quiet, gazing at the floor. I walked away with my heart in my mouth. I put EastEnders on catch-up but a sick feeling had started to rise in my stomach. He sat down and watched TV with me in silence. After the *Duff Duffs*, I switched off the TV and turned to ask what was going on. What I heard felt like a thousand knives through my heart and stomach.

I fell to my knees as he confessed that he had been seeing someone else. My whole body felt trapped in a nightmare and I hoped I would wake up soon. As I struggled to get myself off the floor, he offered no consolation, just silence. I ran to the bathroom and threw up, between wailing and making strange sounds that came from deep within me, almost tribal.

I went back to the sofa, armed with questions. "How have you had time? What's her name? Where did you meet her? Do you love her? How long has it been going on? How old is she? What about us? Where do you go? Where do you do it?" The list went on and on. He answered every question. I laughed out loud at her age; she was 24 and he was 50. She was one of his band's groupies, which made me feel a bit better as surely this was a one-off but, no, it had been going on for a year. He described everything like it was an amazing love story, which was way too much information to give your wife. He said that he felt so much better getting it off his chest and that if I had caught him, he would never have lied to me. Oh, what a hero!

I had never felt so abandoned in my life. Infidelity had hit my family.

To add to the awfulness, he still wanted 'our life' with me and the kids, as well as stay with her. I clearly remember him saying that I should wait until it was out of his system, and that whatever decision happened next was completely up to me. He would just carry on as normal, still seeing her. I was horrified. At that moment, he had stolen my life as I knew it, and the future I thought I had with my family. I felt as though I was staring into an abyss. Alone. All the pressure was now on me to make a choice that would not only affect me but our two young children.

My husband was in a band and played in a London pub a few times a week. I had always been supportive, going to watch him back in the days before our two children were born. We had our dream home and I remember feeling lucky. We even had a dog. Life could not get any better. Of course, the monotony of life, work, kids, appointments, etc could sometimes get me down. He suffered from depression and anxiety, which was hard for us both to deal with at times. We never argued, literally never. We were best friends; we talked about everything and anything. We had dreams of travelling and getting old together. We talked openly and I knew he was frustrated and had missed out on a lot of the 'fun years' in his twenties due to M.E. and other ailments. I am not trying to justify his actions, but I assume that he had compartmentalised his life away from his family and was living a double life.

I was not sure what to do or where to turn. I only told three friends because he said that if I told anyone, then the likelihood of us surviving was slim. It was an emotional threat and my head was a complete mess. We still slept together sometimes and even went away for a weekend. I shudder now to think I did that, but I guess I was trying to save our marriage. This happened just before Christmas. I wrote cards from us both, and we attended parties and two family funerals. I had to sit through family dinners and Christmas Day, pretending. We continued to do the school run, putting on a front by holding hands, while inside I was shrinking.

I spent the next three months in total turmoil. I was utterly broken. I lost weight, which he noticed and joked that I should thank him. What an idiot. I lost friends who sided with him. The friends I had told were amazingly supportive, but I knew that my behaviour frustrated them. "Why haven't you kicked him out? Why haven't you told your mum? What is your plan? What do the children think? Surely you must leave him."

I was overwhelmed, drowning in grief and could no longer see my future. I did not want to be alive. I wanted to be in a dark hole, to hide away and wait for it all to pass. Every day felt like wading through treacle. I had panic attacks, my veins fizzed constantly, my arms felt heavy, I could not sleep and I cried at least 20 times a day. I could not watch TV or listen to the radio. Everything was a trigger. I was exhausted physically and mentally, as my brain was constantly filled with thoughts and questions.

My friends rallied around. They were there for me in so many ways and each had a different style of helping. I highly recommend having a friend who gets angry for you and does all the ranting and shouting, as I was too deep in sadness to feel angry for long. I had another friend who did not judge. She just listened, called every day and cooked for me, even if I could not eat. Another friend took me to the pub and cried with me. She had been through it already, so understood and reassured me that everything was going to be fine. I truly believe that nobody will ever really understand unless they have been through it, and those people are gold. You become sisters, in a way. My friends created a WhatsApp group called 'Sisters of mercy' which was great. They are supporters who recognise your pain because it is all so familiar.

I found a counsellor straightaway and went every week. I hated it at first but slowly started to talk less about him and our past life, and more about what I wanted for my future. Up until then, I had only ever considered what other people wanted and if they were happy. I was frightened of being on my own. In my mind, my husband having an affair was worse than someone dying. I wished he had died because that would have been final and easier to cope with. I remember my mum saying to me, after my dad passed away, "At least he didn't leave me by choice, that would be worse." She was right.

He would randomly turn up at my office and take me for lunch. We would drink wine, have deep conversations and then end up in bed together. Then we would argue as he threatened me not to tell anyone or he would move to Sweden, where he would be welcomed by her family. My head and my heart were at opposite ends. I considered staying and doing nothing but that was torture for me. I kept thinking of our children and my main thoughts were, 'Would I want someone to treat my daughter like this?' and 'What would I tell her to do?' I knew I had to take control and I wanted to drive the situation in my favour.

My counsellor had given me a few lightbulb moments after I had recalled moving to London on my own, having my first weekend job when I was 13, putting myself through university and being financially independent for years. She also made me realise that I had effectively been a single mum for all the time we had been together, and he was the third child I never knew I had.

I needed to pull up my big girl pants!

I finally began to feel empowered and in control of my future. YES…! I was making plans for myself and they did not include him. It took me three months to make that decision. Not that long, considering we had been together for 20 years. I started working out the finances. I had plenty of spreadsheets and knew exactly how much everything was. I was part-time in my job and his earning prospects were higher than mine, so I went to see a divorce lawyer and got my facts straight. I armed myself with knowledge and what I was entitled to. I knew we would have to sell the house. He threatened that he would fight me all the way to get 50:50 but I knew that would cost him, and he would end up worse off.

We sold our house in August 2020 and I filed for divorce on 1st September 2020, on our son's 12th birthday; 18 months after I had discovered his secret. We had lived through lockdown together and survived, but that's another story. I bought a house nearer to my friends, and the kids' school, with enough money to do it up how I wanted. The arrangement is that the kids spend one week at his and one week at mine. They are now 11 and 15 and are the only ones who still suffer disruption of their lives each week. I will never forgive him for that.

The first night in my new house felt amazing. I felt like I was 19 years old again, in my first student digs. As a photographer, I have always had a creative flare. I thoroughly enjoyed designing my home, painting everything myself and being adventurous with the colours and furniture to enhance the interior. All of a sudden, I felt different. The freedom and endless possibilities were no longer scary, but exciting. I was in charge of everything, and it felt good.

I miss what we had. The laughs, the conversations and the good times, but those two people are now gone. He is totally different to the man I first met. His midlife crisis is in full swing and I have been born again into a much better, happier version of myself. I have levelled up, evolved and left the 'beta' version of me behind. I love my life now and wish I could reach out to the 'me' from those awful times, hug her and tell her that it is going to be alright. Just get through the tough bits. Life on the other side of divorce is bloody fantastic.

I sometimes wonder who I would be now, if we had stayed together, or if I had never found out that night. I thought I was happy in my old life, and I would never wish that pain on anyone, but I am excited for the future. I feel 10 years younger and 10 years wiser.

The world is my oyster.

Sarah's Reflections

Feel the nudge. We all have annoyances we put up with for an easier life. You may shrug them off, make do, or not even be aware of them. But when you are forced to deal with a bad situation then everything you tolerated, to keep someone else happy, hits you in the face. Carly had become a dimmer version of herself. She was given the nudge she did not realise she needed and then jumped at the chance to put her life right.

What might you be putting up with?

Improvising. When did you last adapt to circumstances? Probably today or yesterday. Your day did not go to plan, and you had to quickly come up with a solution. Humans have an innate ability to go into survival mode to solve a problem. Your brain is trained to be on full alert. Carly was able to improvise during a difficult time because her survival instinct kicked in.

Remember when. It is amazing how easily we forget times when we have rocked and been totally fab-u-lous. It can take someone asking the right questions for us to see how much fight we still have in us. Carly went to see a counsellor and those lightbulb moments made her impressive character shine. Grab the opportunity, right now. Write down your strengths, so you can see in print what makes you awesome. You could even be daring. Use these as affirmations to reiterate your great qualities and say them out loud as often as you need, until you believe them.

15
Marc Skinner

'Always be yourself' – Al Roker

I was raped on 14th May 1988.
I can still remember every detail vividly.

Family life was hard, as my dad was having a breakdown. He took his anger out on me and I would get a smack most days. Another family member took an overdose in a suicide attempt, after writing letters to all the family. In my letter, a lot of the blame was laid at my door. I found this hard to deal with and needed to escape. As my friends went to the Air Cadets, I followed suit and joined when I was 11.

It was during this time that I met a non-commissioned officer who befriended me and some of the other young cadets. We felt lucky because we went on trips that other cadets did not get a chance to go on. When I was 13, I was taken out by this man and made to feel special.

We went to his friend's house for a BBQ. I was feeling tired, so I went for a lie-down. I woke about an hour later, with a heavy head, and found him on top of me, holding me down whilst he and three of his friends raped me. One had his hand over my mouth so I could not scream, while the others took it in turns to touch and abuse me, as well as keep watch. I could feel something in my mouth and, if I had been able to compose myself, I wish I had bitten down. I could smell their aftershave and feel their breath on my face. My legs were cold and I was aware of a pain but, again, I was too dazed to be fully aware of what was happening.

For an hour and a half, I was subjected to their attacks. I lay there, praying for it to end; for someone to come looking for me, but help never came. Looking back, I believe this had been their plan for the trip all along, to drug me and commit those monstrous acts. Eventually, I found the strength to push them off. When they realised that I was coming round from my stupor and they had had their fun, they left the room and went back to the rest of the guests, as though nothing had happened. In tears, I managed to get dressed, leave the house and, in a daze, make my way home. When I got home, no one was there. I had a hot bath and I did not want to leave the bathroom. For two hours, I just sat in the bath and cried.

I did not tell anyone.

I assumed that, with the issues I already had with my family plus their individual troubles, they would not believe me or even take any notice of the change in my behaviour. So, although the whole experience made me feel ashamed, I justified not saying anything to my parents because my dad would have done something silly, and I felt it was best to keep it to myself.

30 years on, that is one of my biggest regrets. I now realise I should have spoken up.

The next morning, I wanted to forget what had happened so I took my dad's pills, intending to end my life, but I could not go through with it. I caught myself looking in the mirror and decided to never go to the Air Cadets again. It was the hardest decision I have ever made, as it ended my dreams of going into the RAF as a cargo pilot. I was also separated from the friends I had made. I could not bear to listen to the tales they told of their adventures, partly because of what I had lost out on from my ordeal, but mainly because the non-commissioned officer responsible was leading the groups. By not going, I would be safe and away from him.

The whole experience made me feel ashamed. My confidence disappeared and I found it hard to open up and trust people who were nice to me. I was a friendly and outgoing person, but I became withdrawn and found it difficult to build meaningful relationships. My school and work suffered as my anger increased over time, and some of it still lingers today. Over the following few years, I found it hard to trust people and lived in fear of being raped or abused again if I let my guard down. In my darkest hours of despair, I worried that I would become an abuser myself.

At 22, I got a job as a residential social worker in a boys' school for sex offenders who had been abused. I hoped that my experience would offer encouragement so they could rebuild their lives and stay away from mainstream prison. I had a few success stories with them, one of whom I am still in touch with today and am happy to report that he is thriving.

The hardest part about not saying anything is that I had no support to get through the situation. The first time I told anyone about my ordeal was when I was 24. I was sitting in a pub beer garden on a date and we were talking about trust. I opened up to her about how I had a lack of trust in people and had never had a meaningful relationship because I could not let people get close. We ended up having an argument and I blurted out, "Well, you weren't raped at 13!" Although it was not the most suitable place to share this information, getting it off my chest after all those years helped me, but I was not ready to talk about it further.

In 2000, we were married. I started to build a life for myself and we had three beautiful children. I still held the scars of what had happened, and it took having my son to make me realise that I could not let it destroy my relationship with my children.

One evening, my wife and I were out at a bowling alley and, suddenly, I froze. I saw the man who had raped me across the room. I could not speak or move. I then felt a rage like never before and I wanted to hurt him but, instead, I approached him and asked, "Do you remember me?" He replied, "No, who are you?" I politely reminded him of who I was and what he had subjected me to when I was 13 years old. There was no flicker of emotion on his face. I told him to leave before I did something I would regret. He went back to his friends and quickly left. I could not see their faces, but I wondered if any of them were his fellow abusers.

My wife and I divorced in 2013. It was another difficult time in my life, but my priority then was to make sure that I still played a big part in my children's lives.

I found a new partner and was happy for a while. I was able to tell her what had happened. Although she seemed to understand, I found it difficult when she tried to cuddle me from behind. She did not understand why I froze or could only lie a certain way or why I would insist that I cuddled her from behind. We split about seven years later and I went off the rails.

I was living in my car, eating once a week, smoking cigarettes that I found discarded on the ground. All the memories from the previous 20 years kept flooding back. My mental health was at an all-time low, so one day at work I climbed onto the roof and decided that I was going to throw myself off.

At that moment, my son phoned me and said, "Dad, I love you." I stood, with my head in my hands, crying. He had no idea that I was about to end my life, but his call saved me and made me realise that I had something to live and fight for.

I was scared and needed help. The next morning, I checked myself into a psychiatric hospital for a three-day psyche review. I underwent cognitive behavioural therapy, trigger tests and multiple CT scans which found fluid on my brain due to a blockage of the spinal column, a condition heightened by stress. They drained seven pints of fluid from my head which relieved the pressure and helped to reduce my paranoia. I was allocated a therapist who helped me work through the issues caused by that incident all those years ago and we are still in touch.

In 2018, I learned that my abuser had passed away. I went to his funeral as I needed to gain some closure. I found out that he had gone on to abuse 15 other young cadets. Hurt and guilt overwhelmed me and I realised that, if I had spoken up, maybe they would have been spared the same fate. I decided, at that point, that I would share my story with my family and friends. The first person I told was my eldest son, the one who had saved me on that rooftop a few months before. He cried and hugged me as I told him everything about my life because I wanted him to know that, no matter what happened in his life, he could always come to me. I did not want him living in a world where he felt he had no one to turn to.

Now I feel I can focus on the person I have become and, although I still find it hard to build friendships, I have learnt to trust people again. It has taken time but I now realise that, although my abuser took a lot from me, he did not take away who I am as a person. I am known as a cheeky chappie and have always had a great sense of humour, despite everything. For the first time, I feel like the old me. Working on film sets, I get to play lots of different roles and characters, and I have started to find my mojo again.

During the last few years, I have used this experience to focus on my family. I have spoken to my kids about what happened and, although they are teenagers, I have asked them to be open and honest, and encouraged them to talk about anything that is on their minds. They know that I will not judge them and will just listen and be there for them. I always want my children and friends to be able to talk to me about things that are going on in their lives.

In the future, I would like to support other men and help them to understand that being raped should not define you but can make you stronger. Each year, on the date it happened, I make sure that I am busy and not alone. Although I remember it vividly, I use it to be productive.

At the end of 2021, I was performing in a pantomime where I met a woman who I now trust and love. She also makes me feel special. After 30 years, I feel able to be cuddled from behind, which has never happened before. Having spoken to my counsellor, he believes that this is the breakthrough I have been looking for and I can finally put all my guilt to rest.

Sarah's Reflections

Share your truth. Marc is very open about the abuse he suffered, although he admits that he used to bottle it up inside. It took him 13 years to find the courage to say something but, when he did, he was able to peel back the hurt and unburden the trauma that had been damaging him. In our *Knocked Sideways* interview, he shared with me this crucial piece of advice, 'Don't be scared to tell people. If you give stuff power, you lose more than once. It doesn't have ownership of your life.' There is more to life than one moment in time.

It is what you do now that counts. If you let it, the past can haunt you and even send you to a place of no return. The here and now needs to be your focus. Talking to Marc, he is the cheeky chap I knew at school. It pains me to know what he was dealing with then, but it is wonderful to see what he has now. Marc's children are his world and keep him strong. He is proud of the life he has created.

Turn off triggers. Anniversaries can be bleak reminders of something you would rather forget. The trick is to not let dates have control of your future. Marc knows his triggers but recognises how to manage them. The date he was raped is imprinted in his memory, but he makes plans to fill that day with fun and distraction, to ensure he is not alone with his thoughts.

16
Jan Ross

'And in the end, it is not the years in your life that count. It is the life in your years'
– Abraham Lincoln

Being a mum had always been my dream, but other challenges lay ahead.

In my twenties, I craved freedom and lived a lifestyle of dancing and having a laugh. I had many relationships, the men were entertaining and we had good times but, deep in my heart, I knew that they were not right for me and did not have the commitment needed to be a dad.

In my early 30s, my choice of career as a children's nurse, and the commitment it took for university, also distracted me and was my focus. When you are young, you live for the moment, thinking that time is endless and that you have forever to make choices. I think I naively thought it would just happen and everything would turn out fine. But, without realising it as I aged, I unintentionally sacrificed my chance to have my own birth child.

At that point in my life, I faced real grief at not being a mum. The unwelcome visitors of sadness and loss mocked me, as they gnawed away and deepened my sense of loss as a woman. I allowed them to run havoc through my mind, making me unhappy and overwhelmed. It was an emotional time and so heart-wrenching that I had to seek help. Counselling helped me to accept where I was in life.

As I turned 50, I found myself reflecting and feeling the maternal instinct that was still alive inside me. I dared myself to be courageous as I imagined how my life could be different. It was scary and I had to fight thoughts of doubt, block out negativity from well-meaning people and not seek too many opinions. Ultimately, I had to be brave and dive deep into other possibilities of being a parent, which was daunting and exciting at the same time.

I decided to explore adoption and what this could mean for me as a single mature woman. I had a home visit from a social worker who reassured me that I was not too old to apply. Once all my preparation work had been completed, the big day arrived when I sat in front of the panel waiting with trepidation and hoping that I could adopt. A unanimous 'yes' was given. I was ecstatic. I was on my way to becoming a mummy. I have a strong faith in God and always felt peaceful and relaxed about His divine providence on my journey.

During a busy shift at work, I received a message from my social worker to say that she had found a match: a 17-month-old boy. I have no idea how I managed it, but I waited until I arrived home from work to look at his profile. I was bursting with excitement and happiness. I just knew that the beautiful baby looking back at me, with big blue eyes and a cheeky smile, was going to be my little boy. I was later matched to him at a panel and quickly commenced contact with his foster carer. Then, one amazing day, I met him face to face. He was such a happy boy, full of smiles. He even sat on my knee. It was a surreal moment.

My son is my joy, the best gift. I am so grateful to have been given this opportunity to be a mummy to a wonderful boy that I never thought I would have. It has answered my deepest desire as a woman. We have bonded and are beautifully falling in love with each other every day. It is challenging at times and can be a juggle logistically, but I would not change anything for the world. We spent a year together, during my adoption leave from work, having lots of fun as we got to know and trust each other, and we built up a close and loving relationship. I realised, at that point, that I had been given the responsibility to offer him a brand-new start, which changed the course of both our lives. It was remarkable.

I eventually returned to my job as a high-dependency nurse in a children's hospital. I worked one night shift and sadly caught pneumonia. I brushed it off. I was always catching colds from my son, as he was at nursery, but I was admitted to hospital where I stayed for three weeks with a list of ailments. After many tests, I got the results I was not expecting.

I had to absorb and digest the diagnosis of blood cancer.

The unwelcome name of 'Multiple Myeloma'. I had never heard of it. Looking back, I realise that the masterful thing about the human body is that it can freeze information in your mind; some call it denial, non-acceptance or even self-preservation. Over time, I embraced my diagnosis with courage and my family and friends gathered around to help support me along the way. I took it on the chin, so to speak. I call it the 'unwelcome visitor' and I am appalled that this disease has the audacity to wander around my body. How dare it. I prefer to have this attitude as I am not letting it win. It is an imposter I will fight against.

In light of the news, I made a choice to rise above everything tough and overwhelming. I believe there is always a solution, and everything must change as nothing stays the same. My diagnosis is treatable, just not curable right now. On a positive slant, there is a lot of research invested in this form of blood cancer. Treatment has come on in leaps and bounds, and people are living longer and having better quality lives. I am now on second-line chemotherapy treatment which is heading in the right direction. The treatment can be challenging with fatigue and sickness, but I choose to dig deep and get on with it. I am hoping to have a stem cell transplant which should take me into remission and then, after that, I would need maintenance treatment once a month. It all looks positive, which helps me focus on directing myself towards a better future.

My little boy is aware that his mummy goes to the hospital for needles. His favourite thing is pulling my plasters off. He loves watching me squirm, then he pats my arm and says, "Mummy, it's going to be ok." He is too young to understand. I try to keep things light-hearted and playful as much as I can. My son is my heart. He gives my life meaning and helps me focus and look to the future.

My mum is a strong woman who taught my sister and me to be independent, which has given us the fortitude and resilience to embrace life's challenges. I have a strong support system of friends who look after my little boy when I have days of fatigue. They do not treat me any differently and we do not obsess about my illness. They treat me as a strong independent person, which I believe keeps me positive. It keeps my mind in a healthy place and gives me greater courage to fight.

Please, do not get me wrong, I have my moments of sadness, and cry when I need to, but I never allow self-pity to take over. It has tried several times. It used to have a sneaky disguise and I thought that it had come to soothe me, as it stroked my wounds in my moments of vulnerability. But I now recognise how it craftily waits to pounce, sink its teeth into my head, and then pull me down and weaken my fight to be well. I call it out. "You are an imposter and I am not allowing you to be in control." I believe that once you recognise this pattern of emotions, it is the first step to not allowing things to beat you.

My faith in God keeps me grounded and happy, despite everything. I know that His plan for me is to live. My faith journey started in my twenties. I had battled through depression, my life had lost its meaning, and everything seemed dull. A friend told me about Jesus and that life was in Him. It was all foreign to me, but I wanted to exchange the wretched lifeless feelings I had, so I allowed Him to come and live in my heart. Within a short time, my life started to change. It gained colour and I felt alive again. I continue to feel whole and loved through my relationship with Jesus and He directs my path and sustains me. He takes away my fear, gives me strength and I know I can trust Him through this challenging time.

I believe that my son and I will have a long life together. What I dreamed my life would look like is now different, but I have a strong sense of expectation for the future. I aim to be super positive, tackle fear head on and diffuse its power. I have changed into a person who now longs to live in the moment and is open and willing to try new things. Despite all that has happened to me over the years, I have gained great courage.

Life is never a straight path. Challenging times can cause us to think deeply and examine ourselves with sensitivity and honesty. They have helped me adapt to change with greater ease and allowed me to accept the beginning of something new. I have found surprising moments which have reminded me that moving sideways and forwards are both needed to navigate through life. It is like the dance of life; the cha-cha-cha that animates moments of sheer euphoria, which have helped when I have felt stuck and needed to escape. It is only when I have had a chance to look back and reflect that I have seen a solution and, eventually, a different pathway to travel along. It has sometimes not been the one I expected, but there have been beautiful surprises along the way. Life is full of unexpected moments that project you to the place you were always meant to be. Rough moments are needed to reach your destination.

I am strong and courageous and, through difficult times, God gives me strength daily.

What would I like to say to anyone reading this?

Even though life can be tough and unbearable at times, do not give up. Stand and be militant, dig deep, and shout and scream as loud as you can. Refuse to let self-pity win. Hold on to the belief that all is not lost. Live in the moment and try not to become overwhelmed with guilty thoughts and regretful thinking. You can be knocked off course, but it is possible to bounce back and get your life on track. Great expectations are ahead of you.

Since I wrote my chapter, after a drug trial in November 2022 I am now in complete remission. I still take medication but feel much healthier. I am looking forward to the future with hope.

Sarah's Reflections

Our time is not endless. Jan states this important fact. Five words you need to pay attention to. What are you spending time on? What must you start doing? What must you stop doing? We sometimes allow unimportant tasks or others' needs to take priority. You need time for thinking, but you must make time for doing. Time is precious and your biggest asset.

Forever hopeful. Maintaining hope, in any situation, can take all of your inner strength but it will be a crucial part of your coping process. C.R. Snyder, offers essential research into hope and explains that it is the belief in the ability to pursue goals and the development of pathways to reach those goals.

The Hope Scale is a useful tool where you can ask yourself these three questions daily:

- How hopeful do I feel today?

  Rate on a scale of 1 to 10.

- Which factors influence my hope today? Briefly list what contributes to my hope level.

- What small step will increase my hope? Are there any actions or strategies I can take?

Circle of support. Jan found strength and courage in God. Religion is a strong belief for many and can bring light to dark days. Some find sanctuary in spirituality, through nature and a deep sense of connection beyond themselves, and others gain comfort from family, friends, work colleagues or their local community. Reaching out for support means you are not alone.

17

Fiona Setch

'Stop and smell the roses' - Mac Davis

My mum's 81st birthday would be the last day we would spend together.

It was 8th March 2020 at twilight and our friend Linda was with us. We enjoyed flowers, chocolates and birthday cake. There were murmurations of swifts, swooping and gliding in the evening sky, which were spectacular to watch. Mum loved birds and those beautiful sightings over Westerhope had always been her 'WOW' moments. We sat holding hands and enjoyed the dancing sky. I remember thinking if that was Mum's last birthday, what a wonderful time we had together.

My darling mum was an amazing woman. She survived an abusive marriage and became a divorcee in 1968 when net curtains twitched at the sight of a divorced woman. She worked hard as a teacher to bring up my brother and me, whilst caring for her parents who were struggling with my grandpa having Parkinson's disease. As I grew up, Mum was my friend, cheerleader and role model. After her divorce, she struggled with anxiety, loneliness and alcohol dependence until the dreadful brain haemorrhages changed her life at 59.

At 11 pm on 10th June 1997, I sat outside a CT scanner at Newcastle General Hospital, feeling terrified. Having trained as a nurse, with experience of working in a neurology unit, I knew my mum was critically ill. Emergency surgery and weeks of intensive care followed as life and death hung in the balance. It was hard. Yet being able to sit and hold her hand, making sure her room had cards and photographs that showed Ruth, the piano teacher, church organist, mother and holiday carer of our cats, was a real comfort to me. Mum recovered but had a right-sided weakness where she could no longer walk or live independently.

After six months of rehabilitation and discharge planning, we decided to find a new home and adapt it so that she could live the rest of her days with us. We found a lovely house and were able to develop the downstairs for wheelchair accessibility. Her electric wheelchair became her chariot and she learned to glide around the house, click, click, clicking. Carers came in every day to provide the physical care she required and I helped her in the evenings. Not once did I hear her complain, despite her life-changing injuries.

With the independence of a black cab account, Mum would visit Newcastle, enjoying her favourite shop Fenwick, her beauty salon visits, and Waterstones for new books. Our local Theatre Royal had special facilities, enabling us to share our love of musical theatre. Each Christmas, we enjoyed planning our *Festive Extravaganza*, a festive meal to say thank you to people involved in her care during the year.

The original timeframe of six months became 11 years of living with us. "Good morning, mother person" and "Good morning, daughter person" was our ritual as I took her breakfast in bed.

My own journey to becoming a mother was far from easy. Two miscarriages and a lot of upset and stress. My mum helped me through a very emotional time. I had some great advice from a Chinese medicine clinic, "Your yin and yang are out of sync, that is why you are having problems." I was prescribed a warm slimy herb concoction and acupuncture. I finally fell pregnant and my mum was overjoyed. Sharing the joy of Jamie's arrival in April 2004 is a memory I treasure and Mum was such a support to me, helping me adjust to motherhood. She enjoyed every moment of being Granny Ruth and, as Jamie got older, they shared a love of music.

Mum was amazing and grew from strength to strength. It became time for her to try living on her own. Before she moved out, we sat down and had a long chat about our relationship and her future, including her death. We held hands and talked about having a funeral plan. She said she did not want me to have to look after her when she died, as I had looked after her very well during her illness. Having funeral costs planned and taken care of would make it easier. Mum's wishes were simple. She wanted me, her 'darling daughter person', to be with her, knowing that I would be able to care for her, wherever she was. She chose to be cremated, with music and songs to celebrate her life of teaching children music, kindness and being a mother to Sam and me, which were what she described as her most amazing gifts. The music she wanted for her funeral included *Lord of the Dance* and Abba songs, *Dancing Queen* and *Thank You for the Music*, as well as piano playing.

She lived in sheltered housing for a short while, but that flat was not quite right for her electric wheelchair, so we looked around to find her a place in purpose-built sheltered housing with a care project. What a moment when she went into her new open-plan living room and kitchen. "WOW, WOW!" she exclaimed, as she did a big circle in her wheelchair.

Mum lived there for three happy years, going down to the café and sitting with her friends. Sadly, dementia started taking over her life and impinging on our special relationship. The last time we went to the theatre together, to see the singing and dancing spectacular musical *Top Hat*, we sat mesmerised. On our taxi journey home, I asked her what she had enjoyed the most. She took my hand, looked into my eyes, and said, "Holding your hand with the music." Five minutes later, Mum could not remember what we had been to see. It was distressing for her not to be able to remember, so our long conversations about life got shorter until it became me talking, her smiling and saying, "WOW".

Eventually, the carers could not manage her dementia, and it was time for her to move into a nursing home. She lived there for five years. Three days after her 81st birthday, the nursing home went into lockdown due to COVID. That was the last time I held her hand, hugged her, brushed her hair, felt her warmth and heard her voice exclaiming, "WOW" with the wonder of the murmurations. For 22 years, I was her health advocate and was involved in every aspect of her care. I was always able to be there, hold her hand and make sure she was getting exactly what she needed.

Life in lockdown meant I was only able to visit my mum from outside her room in the car park. I would count on the slow walk from my front door to her window... 722 steps.

I visited every day, sometimes twice or three times, just to see her and to know that she knew I was there, although her dementia meant she did not always know who I was, which was tough. I imagined her thinking, "Who is that strange lady who keeps appearing outside my window?" For me, I can only describe it as heart-breaking. It felt cruel. I wanted to break the rules and burst into the home to be with her and hold her hand again.

Tragically, and inevitably, Mum succumbed to COVID and for three long weeks, all I could do was watch her deteriorate. I knew that as she lapsed into unconsciousness, she would still be able to hear the classical music and my voice through the window. She died at 2 am on 2nd May 2020, Week 6 of lockdown and was one of the 322 people who died that day.

After all that we had been through together, with my years of clinical experience as a nurse and then working within palliative care organisations, I was not able to hold her hand, cuddle and comfort her and say goodbye properly. We were not allowed to see her after she died or touch her coffin. The government's COVID rules were very strict. We were only allowed to have eight people at her 20-minute crematorium service, and singing was not allowed. We did have a live stream which allowed people to watch from their homes.

I felt jolted from reality, as my role as her daughter had been ripped from me. My coping strategy was to go into helping mode. Perhaps my experience could help others who were going through similar circumstances. I shared a lot about how I was feeling and coping in Michael Heppell's online Facebook community *How to Be Brilliant* which I was part of. However, I was not dealing with my feelings of loss. Not only was I missing my darling mum, but I was also experiencing many losses: as well as my role as daughter and carer, my work role also evaporated due to the pandemic. I felt lost and empty and unsure of what to do.

Being bereaved during lockdown was hard and the months that followed were a strange new reality. Being denied seeing friends and family, and the physical support of hugs, was immensely difficult. Eventually, I was able to restart work at the hospice. My gym opened and I started to swim again. But I still felt the acute loss of Mum. Not being able to tell her about what was happening in my world; knowing how proud she would have been when Jamie went back to school to collect his GCSE results. I hit a brick wall as Christmas 2020 approached and our country went back into lockdown. The news was full of COVID stories and it seemed impossible to switch off from Mum's death.

An essential part of my recovery was discovering Karen and her role as a soul midwife. Soul midwives are people who provide holistic and spiritual care to people who are dying. I met Karen on Zoom and, through her counselling, she helped me frame the difficulty and tragedy of what I had been through. I realised that I had been suffering from PTSD from only being able to visit my mum outside her nursing home window.

I am lucky to have amazing support around me and I believe this has kept me sane. Hugs, from my husband Koo and son Jamie, are invaluable. As are phone calls, Zoom calls and text messages from my brother Sam and special friends. I find that talking to people makes such a difference, as everyone wants to show encouragement and support. I also find that acknowledging what has happened and writing about my experience helps me let out emotions from deep inside. Something new, since the pandemic, is the opportunity to develop support from the virtual world of *How to Be Brilliant* and TEAM17 communities.

My work gives me great satisfaction and has helped me overcome my feelings of loss. I love making a difference and a contribution to the world through my coaching and training. My personal motto is connected to one of the things I love to do. Wherever there are roses, I enjoy smelling them. It is a simple pleasure that enriches my life. This translates to something I often say to others, 'Always make time to smell the roses in your life.' If COVID taught me anything, it is to appreciate life, right here, right now!

I am learning to live with the new shape of life without my mum, which is forever evolving.

When my mum, Ruby Talby, came home from hospital in 1997, we expected her to live for six months. That became 22 years and remembering those rich experiences is a gift.

The Angel of the North is a sculpture that stands tall and proud by the A1 motorway, quietly contributing to the Northeast, a place Mum and I enjoyed visiting. My mum was my guardian angel and I feel her presence every day. Being her carer was my privilege.

Sarah's Reflections

You cannot control everything. Fiona's words rang in my ears after our *Knocked Sideways* interview. Grief can take you to an unknown place as you are forced to face your biggest fears. You want to control what is happening, but you are unable to. It is not a nice feeling. You feel helpless and hopeless, but focusing on what you can control can make a profound difference.

Learning to live differently. Fiona's life was shattered when her mum died. The loss of a loved one can be crippling and it can be hard to imagine life without them. With the right support, Fiona was able to find a gradual acceptance, so she could turn her pain into purpose. When you deal with loss, it is sadly inevitable that life will be different, but you can still pay tribute and keep them close to you, to find comfort however you feel is best.

Find your WOW. This can be an experience or event that lights up your day and leaves a lasting impression. Fiona brings a rainbow of colour into the world by helping others, always giving, sharing knowledge, breaking into song and creating WOW moments, like her dear mum. When did you last have a WOW moment? How can you add more WOW into your life?

18
Indira Mahun

'There is a light at the end of every tunnel.
Some tunnels just happen to be longer than others'
– Ada Adams

The word 'freedom' did not exist in my family.

For as long as I can remember, my life choices were dictated by my parents. As children, we did as we were told. We listened and we obeyed. But children grow up, become individual human beings, want their own voice and are no longer an extension of their parents. They have their own dreams and ambitions. They become independent or, at least, harbour the yearning to be independent.

At 18, I started to want more freedom, which is when my life took a drastic turn. I fell in love with a boy and, worse still, he was a different colour to me. My dad was livid. This was not allowed and in my parents' eyes, I ceased to exist. They no longer had three daughters and I was erased from their lives. Believing my life would not be worth living, I ran away.

I lived away from home for three years and then disaster struck. A boat trip led to a horrific accident and my boyfriend tragically died. The decision to go swimming in the River Thames took a tragic turn, as a crippling cramp in his leg led him to drown. He had so much to live for and he did not get a chance to fulfil his dreams. I blamed and tortured myself, believing that I could have helped him. I was devastated but there was no one to see my tears or wipe them away. I was angry with myself for the choices I had made. I was only 21, but I had a decent job and managed to complete my A-Levels through all the madness.

I do not blame my parents. It was hurtful and upsetting but I believe they acted in a way that was expected of them at the time. Expectations that arise from the confines of a community and culture must be met or you face the risk of being shunned and ridiculed. Asian families can be unforgiving and, in my experience, lack the capacity to see beyond the visual picture.

I wanted to go home, but that seemed impossible.

Somehow, my parents heard of my misfortune. They came to find me and I became a member of my family again. I never understood why my parents welcomed me back. I believed that I had committed an unforgivable act and yet, there I was, sitting in the house I had deserted. I was in awe of my parents' generosity. The topic was closed. However, the rest of the Asian community was not so forgiving. Consequently, the next logical step for me was to find a husband. It would zip the mouths of the gossipmongers who could find nothing better to do.

Dad found a suitable match. We waited for them to arrive and carry out the Roka ceremony. I sat upstairs in my room, adorned in an Indian outfit. Arranged marriages were the norm and it was the least I could do, as I felt I owed my parents, but the family cancelled because someone had interfered and told them what I had done. Blood boiling, I came to a decision. Although I was not keen on the idea of marrying a stranger, I knew it would make my parents happy and allow them to be a part of the community that had spurned them.

“Mum, Dad, I’m going to India to get married.”

In India, after a quick introduction and engagement, I was married to a man I met once, aged 23. Nonetheless, I felt happy and content, and the stranger soon became the man I loved. He was handsome, funny, understanding and intelligent. He was all I could ever have hoped for in a husband. God gifted us with three beautiful boys. They were, and still are, my world.

About eight years into our marriage, things changed. We arrived back in England and my husband had to find a job. He was no longer his own boss and, instead, became a worker. He could not bear to take orders from people younger and less qualified, so he sought consolation in alcohol. It was then that sadness was thrust upon our family. Drinking became a huge problem. A contender for my love, affection and attention. I found myself drowning in misery.

Alcohol addiction is an illness that can destroy lives. I cared for my husband unconditionally, but my mental state was being compromised. Everyone in my family told me to leave him and even my parents said they would support whatever decision I made. In the beginning, I believed he wanted to give up drinking for good, but I got tired of visiting him in rehab clinics with the same story. He would come out sober, saying, "I promise I won't do it again." Then I would spend every moment looking over my shoulder, waiting for the inevitable.

My husband's addiction ripped through our family and tore us apart. Outsiders offered advice and some had the audacity to question me. No one can understand what goes on behind closed doors. His actions had a domino effect on the choices our children made. Unable to cope with life at home, they turned to other means of survival. I was too wrapped up in trying to deal with my problems to see what was happening to them. Immersed in addictive substances, my boys' lives started to spiral out of control. I felt I had failed as a mother.

One day I woke, bolt upright. I cannot explain why that day was different, but I had a strong urge to do something. I realised that if I carried on like this, my life would be over, and my children would be affected forever. I wanted to enjoy life but, most of all, I wanted to be me again. I had lost myself. I felt I did not exist and I desperately wanted my freedom.

Enough was enough.

I woke up that morning and knew I could no longer help my husband. My boys had suffered because I had taken my eyes off them for too long. My husband had to leave our family home. I would miss him, but he was not the man I married or loved anymore. It was the only way I could protect my family and bring normality back into our lives. I could not bear to throw him out onto the streets as I would not be able to forgive myself if anything happened. I knew he could never survive on his own. He had family in India, and it was where he had been happiest.

Did he protest? He may have, but he did not object. I took him for his visa photograph whilst he was drunk. I told him where he was going but he stared at me blankly. He slept in the car on the way to the airport. Once there, he needed my support to get through departures. I asked an airport assistant to make sure he got onto the plane. The minute I knew he had boarded, my stress floated away. A weight had been lifted and I felt light and giddy.

It helps to have someone to talk to. I poured my heart out to work colleagues who did not judge. They were always there to listen and provide a shoulder to cry on. My family were my rock. Although divorce is frowned upon in Asian communities, my parents supported me.

My husband did not want us to divorce and I knew he was sad leaving everything we had built together. I hoped the break would make a difference but his drinking continued in India. Our phone conversations were difficult. He often sounded confused and would lash out and call me names.

My mind was made up. I needed to divorce him.

My children knew that my decision was the right one and they were with me all the way. They had shared my misery and knew that we could not continue together. They had witnessed the constant fighting, arguing, vomiting and the smell of alcohol, so never said they missed him.

Sadly, my husband passed away 10 years ago. He was only 50. A wasted life because he had made the wrong choices. My family survived because I made the right decision.

Of course, it is not only the addicted who need help but also the partners and families who suffer alongside them. There is a lot of help available from various agencies and I was able to get the right support by being honest with my GP about my concerns.

I had wasted so much time being unhappy and I had to do something for myself. Love and affection were feelings I did not recognise anymore, and I had no confidence. I was also worried about what my children thought of me, but they reassured me. "Mum, you must do what makes you happy. If you meet someone else, we do not mind. We haven't seen you smile for so long," they said. They gave me the strength and courage to move forward.

Online dating was the only way I could see myself meeting anyone. It was a big step and tested my faith in men again, but I knew I was ready for new beginnings and a new relationship where I could take control of my life. The first date went well and we agreed to meet again. My confidence was restored and I was determined to put the past behind me. We have now been in a loving relationship for ten years. As they say, "It's never too late."

My resilience and power come from my children. They are my hope and strength and give me all the reasons I need to live. A secure and loving home helped them to stabilise their lives and realise their potential. They have fought hard but have come through the other side with smiles and successes. I am extremely proud of my boys Harpal, Gurpal and Lakhpal and I can now focus on them. All three of them are married to girls who are like daughters to me, and I have been blessed with two beautiful granddaughters. I'm the happiest I have ever been.

God has always been my strength. I wholeheartedly believe that everything happens for a reason and that God has a plan for all of us. Yes, we make our own choices, but they are the choices we are guided to make. My faith and prayer got me through many a dark time.

I had given up writing, which had always made me happy. I write as much as I can now. Writing completes me. I read a lot and find solace, hope and peace in books. There is much we can learn from reading and there is nothing quite like losing yourself in a different world.

I have learnt how to believe in myself. The decision to force my husband to leave and finally divorce him was the hardest one I have ever had to make. At that moment, I threw caution to the wind and put myself first. I remember thinking, "Sod the lot of them. It's my life and I am the one who has to live in this hell, day-in-day-out."

It is important to be courageous, take control and not always do things to please others. I feel strong and more empowered. It is my life and I will live it, making the best decisions for me.

Sarah's Reflections

Awaken awareness. Self-worth starts with a foundation that is built from a combination of factors. Indira talks about a lack of freedom from a young age and 'not existing' while she was married. All of a sudden, she had an innate awareness to take control and break free. You must recognise your inherent value as an individual and that you deserve love, respect and happiness.

Avoid permanent 'ouch'. When you dread waking up every day, something is wrong. Setting an intention is a great way to take control. You might want a simple daily goal, or one you would like to achieve in the future. The question is, what must you do to get there? When you live with intent it prompts you to be present so you can focus on what genuinely matters and avoid distractions. Flick that switch and lean into it.

Vision is the ignition. Just as a car needs fuel to start, you need inspiration to initiate your journey throughout life. Indira visualised her happiness, and a stable life for her sons, which served as the motivation she needed to take the first step to a new life. Are you heading in the right direction? It can be overwhelming, but taking small steps can lead to a big change.

19
Ray Vincent

'Don't ask yourself what the world needs. Ask yourself what makes you come alive, and go do that'
– Howard Thurman

I cannot look back on a specific day and say that one moment changed my life.

My story is more of a gradual coming to terms with a fact that would have a deep effect on my whole life – the realisation that I am homosexual.

It was the only word I knew at the time, before the term 'gay' would mean what it does today. In the working-class world, in which I grew up, the subject was hardly mentioned; even the boys in school who were always telling dirty jokes did not really know what it meant. I enjoyed the closeness and special friendship with boys and assumed that everybody felt the same. Even the naughty thoughts I had about male bodies did not seem unusual when I observed some of the horseplay my schoolmates got up to.

As I came into my late teens, I started to wonder whether I was different. Boys were talking about the things they did with girls or, at least, the things they would like to do with them. I just did not find girls, or that kind of thing, interesting. In those days, before the Pill and the cult of sexual freedom, it was rare for teenagers to have sex. There was only what was called 'snogging'. In my innocence, I began to wonder why I was not attracted to girls and thought perhaps it was like smoking or drinking. If you had never done it, you could not understand what people saw in it, but once you got into the habit, you were hooked.

Then one day, when I was about 17, I came across the word 'homosexual' in a magazine article. I had seen it before and assumed that it meant something a bit dirty or perverted but, this time, I was curious to know what it really meant. I looked it up in a dictionary and immediately it struck me, 'That's what I am.' I felt it was both good and bad news. Good news because, if there was a word for it, then I would not be the only one who had those feelings, and bad news because it seemed to be something wrong and abnormal.

It was about that time that a change was happening in my religious experience. I had been brought up in a church-going family and had accepted Christianity but, as an adolescent, I began to doubt it. I was enthused by the great poetry and literature I was reading in school, but the teachings I heard from sermons and Sunday School seemed dull and restrictive by comparison. It was through poetry, and especially by reading Browning under the influence of G. K. Chesterton's book about him, that I suddenly saw a different, fresh way of saying the same things as the Christian faith. It was an exciting discovery, and there came with it a sense of calling to become a minister. But there was the catch. How could I be an open homosexual and a minister? I knew I would have to live a celibate life.

From then on, I avidly read everything I could to find out about homosexuality, in secret of course. I felt too ashamed and afraid to talk with anyone else about it. In my reading, I discovered the theory that most adolescents go through a homosexual stage and eventually grow out of it. I even had a girlfriend for a time and felt quite proud of myself. I was just like other boys after all. But eventually, I realised that my attraction to boys was not a passing phase. It was a permanent fact about me and could not be denied.

There were times when I felt my loneliness was a burden, but I learned to find strength in my Christian faith. For me, the essence of the Christian message has always been God's unconditional love. Whoever we are, whatever we have done or not done, and whatever others think of us, we are creatures of God, loved and accepted. In any case, I do not ever remember thinking that my sexuality was wrong in the sight of God. My faith is not a fundamentalist one and I regard the few things the Bible says about homosexuality as the thoughts of an ancient culture which were very different from our own. I believe they have nothing to do with genuinely loving consensual relationships between people of the same sex.

I have been celibate most of my life, not because I think my sexual desires are sinful, but for other reasons. One is my commitment to being a minister and, though things have changed, for many years the kind of relationship I wanted would have meant living with a secret. That would have affected my integrity and got in the way of my relationship with the church.

The other factor was my love and respect for people. I have spent a lot of time with young men and have felt sexually attracted to many of them. However, either they were not gay, or the circumstances were such that it seemed inappropriate to look for that kind of relationship with them. What held me back was not fear of being punished by God, but respect for my friends. I did not want to do anything that would worry or embarrass them; their friendship was more important than sex.

One thought that sustains me is that the love I feel, even if unrequited, is part of the love of God and brings me closer to him. My favourite prayer is attributed to St Francis, 'Let me not seek as much to be consoled as to console, to be understood as to understand, to be loved as to love.' I have proven the saying of Jesus, 'Give, and you will receive.' If we approach people with genuine love, it is wonderful to see how much love there is all around us.

Some people take the risk of coming out at an early age. Others never come out at all and take their secret to the grave. I come between the two extremes. For many years, I kept my feelings to myself and was terrified of anyone suspecting my real nature. If the subject ever came up in conversation, I suffered excruciating embarrassment. From time to time, I fell in love with other men. I made up all kinds of excuses to spend time with them, but I never dared to show them my real feelings.

The first person I came out to was a woman. It was in my early days as a minister. I was a student chaplain and Patricia was one of the students. She was down-to-earth and sensible. We were amused and annoyed by the same things, and we each seemed to know what the other was thinking. It felt like a pleasant easy-going friendship but, after a few months, I started to realise that she was looking for more than that. It was not the first time a girl had shown feelings towards me, but I had always dodged out of the situation with excuses. I could not do this with Patricia because I liked and respected her too much. I knew the time would come when I had to tell her the truth.

It came one night when we were at a birthday party. After the usual food and drink and some dancing, people were beginning to pair off for a bit of kissing and cuddling, and I felt trapped. As we were dancing together, Patricia remarked how hot it was in the room. Seizing the opportunity, I suggested that we went for a walk. As we walked around the chilly streets, I mustered up the courage to tell her the truth. I had no idea how she would react, but she took it well and we remained friends. I was 30 years old, and it was the first time I had told my secret to another living soul.

The next person I came out to, about six years later, was a man I was in love with. He was another minister, a married man with children. We had been students together and close friends for a long time. I longed to share my secret with him – not to come between him and his wife, but just so that our friendship could be more honest. There came a weekend when we were together at two back-to-back conferences. But the whole four days went by and somehow my chance never came. When I got home, I was so furious with myself that I felt the only thing I could do was to sit down and write him a long letter, telling him the whole truth. At the post box, I held the letter in my hand for a moment and thought, 'This is an action that's going to change my life.' I dropped it in. It did change my life – for the better. My friendship with him, and with his wife, became deeper and more open from then on.

As the years went by, I came out gradually to a few more friends. Some of them challenged and encouraged me to come out publicly, but it was a slow process. As I was still living a celibate life, I felt no pressure to come out. I never had to face coming out to my parents, as they had both died young. In my sixtieth year, I had the experience most people have in their teens. I fell in love, had a whirlwind romance, and had my heart broken.

Things have changed a lot in many churches. In my later years as a minister, I did not hide my views about homosexuality. Some people in my church supported me and, although some disagreed, they were gracious. The only opposition came from other churches. The church I joined after retirement is exceptionally open and inclusive. At the age of 80, I had the opportunity to stand up in front of a congregation and tell my story for the first time. The reception they gave me was heart-warming and included a celebration cake. I also became a university chaplain and ended up running the LGBT staff network. Thanks to some members who nominated me, I was named Stonewall's Gay Role Model of the Year in 2019. This was exciting and slightly scary. I was featured in the national press and on the radio. The award opened more doors for me to talk and write. Looking back to the time when I was terrified that anyone should even suspect I was gay, it all seems unbelievable.

Coming out is a personal business, and no one should be put under pressure. I claim no credit for it. Others have been far more courageous, and I might never have come out if I had not had the encouragement of friends. I came out at a time when it was much easier but, for many people, it is still difficult and in some parts of the world it can cost people their families and even their lives. For me, I have found a new sense of freedom and connection with people. My only regret is that I did not come out sooner. Now I want to make up for lost time by doing all I can to make the way easier to support others.

I have set up a website www.freetoloveandbelieve.com where I share my passions and post regular blogs.

In my youth, I saw my sexuality as a cross to bear. Later, I came to accept it and now I enjoy it as a gift and a privilege, even as a calling. Being open about my sexuality is not always easy or comfortable, but it brings the deep satisfaction of knowing that I am in the right place.

I am finally being who I was born to be.

Sarah's Reflections

A lightbulb moment can strike at any time. Ray's story highlights that being *knocked sideways* does not have to be instant. As you grow older, wiser and develop a level of confidence and independence, you naturally start to question elements of your life. Then, all of a sudden, you know. It is empowering to choose the right path, the one you were destined to walk.

Do you ever think you are living, but not as the real you?

Do you behave a certain way due to others' expectations?

It is liberating to be true to yourself and Ray writes beautifully about this.

Be curious. Ray was brave enough to be curious about his sexuality. He was keen to understand his inner feelings. When you look deeper to find answers it can be rewarding. Introspection is often necessary to interpret and connect with our true selves.

What makes you curious?

Have you questions that are yet to be answered or an urge worth exploring?

Keeping faith. Ray's unwavering belief in God played a pivotal role in sustaining him through loneliness and pressures of coming out as a gay man. Having faith can provide you with a powerful source of love and offers guidance towards your journey of self-acceptance. How do you keep your faith? It can be religion, or you may hold a different belief system. Whatever you choose is brilliant, as long as you continue to nurture how you grow as an individual.

20
Kathleen Findlay

'I think I can, I think I can…'
The Little Engine That Could – Watty Piper

My mum took her own life when she was 40. I was 15. We learnt later that she had been bipolar, self-harmed and was a manic depressive who had made several suicide attempts.

Shortly afterwards, my older brother and sister moved out and my younger brother, who was 13, and I became immensely close. We understood what each other was thinking and feeling.

Surprisingly, I managed to get through school. Incidentally, my dad never told the school that my mum had died. He did not share or talk about things at all. We were a Catholic family and suicide was a criminal offence until 1968 and a bit taboo. We carried on as normal with few people knowing. My mum had told me, "You'll manage without me, you'll cope" and so I did. My dad, brother and I stuck together. Life was tough, but we had each other.

I coped by pretending everything was fine, shutting out what had happened so that I could protect myself. I thought it best not to say anything to anyone, so I kept quiet and buried my feelings deep inside my metaphorical 'black bag'. I used to be afraid to think. I would shake my head and say, "I won't think about that just now." The trouble was, I would hold it in for over 30 years.

Pretending

Pretending – I'm good at that, it's really easy
Nobody notices because I'm so breezy
I hear them say "She's doing well"
I'm good at pretending nobody can tell
The face is on the smile fixed
Nobody knows my little tricks
Why do I pretend I'm okay?
Suppose I've never known any other way
It's easier to pretend every day
Then I don't get in anyone's way
I'm okay, I'm fine that's how it goes
Easy-peasy

I met my husband James at school, and we married in 1984. We were happy, we had two children and I continued to work full-time in HR. In 2004, James was working in Baku

(Azerbaijan) when he died suddenly of a hereditary heart attack. The police knocked on my door on Mother's Day to tell me the tragic news. It was a great shock as he was only 45.

My world was turned upside down. My dad was there for me when my husband died. I remember him just sitting with me holding my hand, he did not need to say anything. Then 18 months later, my younger brother was killed in a motorbike accident. I was numb for a long time and did not know who to grieve for. I went back to work part-time a few months later as I needed to support my son (12) and daughter (15). The support of friends was invaluable. People asked how I was coping, but I felt I had no choice as I just had to get on with it. My mantra was 'one day at a time' and if I could get up each day and wash my face it was an achievement. I went to Cruse who offered bereavement counselling and the woman I was allocated was nice, but she offered tea and sympathy and I wanted much more. I searched for books on multiple deaths to understand if I was grieving correctly. I wanted to talk to people who had been through several losses; not to compare, but to find some reassurance that I was not going mad.

I went on a coaching weekend which I believed was going to be relaxing, but that was where I took the first step and delved into my 'black bag' where I had hidden everything. I came away totally wiped out and scared but realised I needed to find a way to release my emotions.

Two months later, I made the decision to see a psychotherapist and had nine sessions. I had not talked about my mum's death for 30 years. I was told that I was exhausted from coping and that if I did not do something about it, it would affect my ongoing health. I discovered that I held everything in my stomach. A few years ago, I went to see a spiritual response therapist who worked with me to release emotions by massaging my stomach. It was a strange experience but it worked, and I sobbed like never before. My advice is to find someone to talk to as you cannot keep hold of those emotions, worries and concerns.

I have learnt that there is no correct way to grieve. You must work through it yourself. I had found it difficult to articulate my emotions. I once found a book about loss called *Eternal Echoes* by John O'Donohue, which described my feelings exactly. I had been writing poetry since I was a young adult but never showed it to anyone. When I could not express my feelings verbally, I seemed to be able to write about them and it was reassuring that no one would see them. Often, I was not aware of what I was writing, the words just came out.

Talking

Everything jumbled tumbling out

Trying to make sense of the stuff I spout

Down through the head through my arm

On to the page

Just let it flow, get rid of the rage

Emotions and feelings spitting out

It's better than raving and wanting to shout

Just shut your eyes and let it flow

The ink will tell you what you need to know

Whilst doing consultancy work, I saw a poster about a charity walk for the Inca Trail in Peru. Machu Picchu was a place James had always wanted to visit. Some friends had gone there the year before and built a cairn for him with stones from the beach where I live in Scotland. In October 2007, I completed the trail and raised £4,500 for the British Heart Foundation. It was an amazing experience and hugely emotional. It is a spiritual place, and it was there that I was able to let out a lot of my grief. I was given the privilege of being the first through the sun gate and was asked to close my eyes, setting the scene. I stepped through and had a spiritual moment at the end of the journey. The whole experience helped me to heal.

The Sun Gate

Stop, right here at the top of the steps

Come to the front the one who's upset

Stand right here and close your eyes

Gather your thoughts and all of those ties.

I have walked for miles carrying my load

I'm so weary and tired of this road

Can I let go when I step through the gate?

It's time to see the sun it is my fate

You're here now this is it

Lost in an aura of the spirit

The tears I shed were for everything lost

But you were there when I looked across

High up in the hill, a fleeting movement

Was enough for me that precious moment

"You're done" whispered in the breeze

It was a glimpse, a moment I wanted to freeze

But then gone, fleeting back to your place nothing left no sign or trace.

But in my heart, it is tucked away
That brief moment you came to say
"Move on now, it's time to go
Take care and remember I love you so"

In November 2008, I returned to Peru and worked with a community at a school in the Andes, building chimneys and planting fruit trees. I stayed for a month, and it was one of the happiest times I had had for a long time. There were a lot of social problems and the children did not get a lot of hugs, so to get one was special. It is so rewarding to help others. I would recommend it. When you are busy looking after others, you do not have time to dwell on your own problems.

I was brought up as, and still am, a practising Catholic. I think my belief in God has helped, believing that those I have lost have gone to a better place and that I will see them again.

Through my loss, I did quite a bit of reflection which was unusual for me, but what I struggled with the most was 'Why did I have to lose all these people?' What I learnt was that I needed to accept what had happened, as this sadly is a part of life. It took me a while to accept my new life without my husband and to start thinking about what I wanted for my future.

During that difficult time, my son had gone slightly off the rails and was hanging around with the wrong crowd. I ended up collecting him from the police station one night. I needed to do something, and I felt the best solution was to send him to a boarding school 70 miles away. It was the most difficult decision I had ever had to make, and I asked many people if I was making the right choice. A friend suggested that I see a CBT coach, and that really helped. We talked through my worst fears, the main one being that my son would be so unhappy that he would take his own life. She made me realise that if things got bad then I could bring him home. I knew at the end of the session I was doing what was right for my son.

I now make sure I grasp opportunities because, if you wait, you might not do them. In 2007, I was picked by *Psychologies Magazine* to do Fast Therapy with Benjamin Fry and each time I tried to explain how I felt I read one of my poems. Benjamin asked me what I would call my anthology of poems if I put them together and I said *Help*. I wanted to scream at people and say, "I'm not okay. I need help." I had a slight panic attack when he first asked me to share my poems, as he was asking me to bare my soul, but now I am selling my little book of poems called *Help* for the charity *Cruse*. I have had amazing feedback and people say that my poems help them so much. They can relate to the words, and it makes them feel normal.

I was asked to speak at a conference on *Resilience in Adversity* which took me out of my comfort zone, but it made me realise how much I have dealt with in my life. I have been interviewed on TV and radio about living with loss and grief. Each time I share and give a little of myself it makes it easier to move on; each moment can be healing. A friend once gave me good advice to accept every invitation, as you can always go home if it is too much.

I have now learned not to bottle things up and am much more open about my feelings. I still find it difficult to show my vulnerability and asking for help is difficult. But I am forever evolving.

I have always loved to be busy and can see that filling my life, connecting and socialising with others has made such a difference to me. I always encourage people to open their minds and try things that might help. I did all sorts of things: retreats, therapy, counselling, volunteering, Sudoku and crosswords. I found my love for walking and achieved many routes including The West Highland Way, St Cuthbert's Way and The Camino de Santiago. It was not one thing that helped, but an accumulation of many. I found my love for poetry when I was 23 and I still write.

Every day I continue to work on myself and learn new things.

Sarah's Reflections

Help, I need somebody! How often do you feel like this? You play out scenarios in your mind to convince yourself that either you ARE fine, or that you will be judged and made to look stupid if you show any vulnerability. It is good to talk and I promise there will always be someone to listen. Of course, you have to make the first move, which can be scary. But as soon as the words leave your lips, there is an immense feeling of relief. There is no shame in asking for help.

Slow, slow, quick, quick, slow. You can dance through life, but it is important to choose your own pace. One day at a time was what Kathleen needed after experiencing unimaginable loss. Taking things slowly allowed her time to rebuild, connect and understand what gave her pleasure. You can go quickly when you have energy and then slow down when necessary.

To remember to slow down, use the acronym **RESCUE**.

Relax

Escape

Self-**C**are

Understand

Emerge

Accept every invitation. When your world has come crashing down, all you want to do is hide, close the curtains and switch off your phone. Then you realise, that what felt like a few days was actually a week. You do not have the headspace to make decisions, your planning brain has stopped performing and basic day to day living is a puzzle. When we lose someone, support is often there at the beginning but, after the initial month, people start to drift away. Accept offers of help and try to limit 'No' as the answer to an invitation, as they will lead you closer to finding your feet again.

21
Shaun Greenaway

'We didn't come this far to only come this far'
– Matthew Reilly

In 2017, after 8 years of being together as just the two of us, my wife Jenna and I started trying to conceive, to grow our family and begin the next chapter of our lives. Having no success, we went to the doctors to discuss our concerns. Following initial tests, it was established that I had Azoospermia–no sperm in my semen. The doctor explained that it was most likely due to having mumps as a young adult. I also had a large varicocele, which is a cluster of enlarged veins above the testicles and creates problems with sperm production.

I underwent two operations to hopefully try to rectify this. The first was a varicocele embolization which is considered a relatively non-invasive procedure. Following the operation, there was a three-month wait to see if my sperm production had improved. We nervously waited. One day, Jenna was driving me to the train station as I headed off to work and, just as she was parking, the phone rang. The results of the post-varicocele operation sperm test had come through... still no sperm. That was a real blow. Although the chances of the operation improving my count were slim (around 30%), we are inherently positive people and we were hopeful for good news. I guess the flip side to being hopeful and positive is that there is further to fall on the other side, but I certainly would never want to change my outlook on life.

Jenna cried and I was just numb. Frozen even. But I was not sure why. Embarrassment? Shame? Guilt? All of them, I think. We had already chosen an IVF clinic and had been for preliminary appointments; they were just waiting for the outcome of my varicocele operation as it would determine what kind of treatment we would need. Now there was absolutely no doubt about it. If we were going to have a family with Jenna carrying a baby, it would have to be via IVF. This meant that she would have to go through a hell of a lot emotionally and physically, all because of me. Had I failed her? Would she leave me? These were some of the many questions going around my head.

The second operation was a microsurgical testicular sperm extraction (aka Micro-TESE) which was more invasive. This involves an incision into the scrotum, and the outer layer of one testicle is then opened. The surgeon then examines the testicle under a high-powered microscope for any areas containing sperm, and any present are harvested. It was a much bigger procedure, with more potential risks, such as pain, bleeding, infection, low testosterone and, in rare cases, severe testicular damage. I was apprehensive but determined as I wanted to try every avenue. After the operation, I was wheeled back to the ward and, not long afterwards, the surgeon and a nurse came to see us.

No sperm were found.

The results left me lost. I started to question my masculinity and my role as a husband. I wanted to speak to other men in the same situation. Male infertility has been a taboo subject for too long because men are taught to 'man up and get on with it' and suppress their emotions. I did not know anyone who had faced anything like this and could not find any forums of other men going through the same experience. I felt alone and went inward.

I believe that grieving is associated with death, and infertility is a type of death. Not being able to create the picture of the family you always wanted and to pass on your genetic identity. It is only now, on reflection, that I realise that I was unconsciously experiencing the classic stages of grief.

Finding acceptance was a more active practice. A wilful and courageous action, which boils down to choice. To come to terms with something that has happened that cannot be changed. It is key to recognise that this does not mean that you *like* what has happened but you just choose to make space for it in your life. You permit yourself to be who you are and stop expending energy by resisting it. I realised my energy could be better spent supporting Jenna during the next phase of us trying to have a child.

This acceptance also allowed me to reflect on the earlier questioning of my masculinity. Was I still a man if I could not provide sperm? Of course, I was. A journey of infertility gives you a new sense of manliness. Being engaged in your actions, showing up, being there in the tough times and at the tough appointments. The clinics and procedures may be awkward and embarrassing but, by consistently being by your partner's side, showing strength, compassion and love, you are being every bit the man she needs you to be.

I read an incredibly powerful book *The Little Big Things* by Henry Fraser. It is an inspirational story of how he accepted his new reality, following a tragic life-changing accident. He writes about finding gratitude in the simplest of things; things that he would have previously taken for granted. The book led me to reflect on my circumstances. I downloaded an app called *Day One* and, every morning, began writing down what I was grateful for. There have been many studies on the benefits of practising gratitude. It is said to open new neuro pathways in your brain and has numerous positive effects on both mental and physical health.

My wife and I decided that we still wanted to have children, no matter what it took. I knew that I had a lot more to pass on to a child, other than my DNA. My values, my strength, my love and my life experiences. It occurred to us that every vision, every hope and every aspiration we had for the future involved children, so we knew that we would keep on fighting for this dream. We did not want to live a life childless and, although we loved being called 'favourite aunt/uncle', these were not titles that we would be content with.

We wanted to be Mum and Dad.

When it comes to trying to conceive, you are told so much about the importance of physical health. It is easy to see why, as there is such a big emphasis from fertility practitioners on physical aspects, such as a patient's BMI, whether or not they smoke, their diet, and other lifestyle choices such as alcohol intake and an emphasis on taking supplements to assist. I honestly believe that mental health and a positive mindset are just as important. Your mind is a muscle and, like the muscles in your body, it can be made stronger. When keeping fit, you need to follow up with proper recovery time. It is no different with the mind. We often have to deal with many mental stresses and tension, and rest is vital otherwise you can burn out. Trying to conceive can become all-consuming, so it is important to find distractions and still have joy in life. This will allow you to come back stronger for the next phase.

A positive mindset is likely to cope more effectively with a setback. Rather than dwelling on what has happened, you look for ways to continue to move forward. It is well known that negative emotions narrow your focus and thinking, whereas seeing things positively helps open the mind to possibilities. Researchers continue to explore the benefits of positive thinking with some of the advantages being increased immunity, lower levels of stress, better resilience and increased well-being. These are all invaluable when trying to conceive.

My journey of self-discovery set me on a path of wanting to constantly improve myself in every aspect, both physically and mentally. The Japanese use the phrase 'Kaizen' which means 'continuous improvement'.

By focusing on the positives in my life, I was able to acknowledge my strengths and utilise them to overcome adversity. I found a power within myself that allowed me to accept my present and write a new future. After all, you cannot create hope for the future when you are staring into the past, wishing for what could have been.

Once we had mentally processed our situation, my wife and I had to decide which route we would take to become parents. We elected to use donor sperm to continue our journey. This entailed working our way through an extensive list of donor characteristics, whilst my wife had blood tests to establish her Rhesus (Rh) blood group. Once the blood screening was complete and overlaid with our selected criteria, we were matched to six donors.

Each donor form gave vital statistics, height, weight, eye colour, place of birth, ethnic group, etc. It also stated their medical conditions and if they had proven fertility. There was an optional section, where the donor could describe why they were donating, a bit about themselves and any goodwill messages. Only two had written any kind of bio. One was brief, but the second had written a lovely message. It included information about his personality and his family dynamics. We initially found ourselves drawn to this donor, as the bio humanised him. But we did not select him. We decided we did not want to know too much about the donor. We wanted a blank canvas, so to speak. In the end, the donor we chose had provided the bare minimum of information. His statistics were all within normal ranges, with no medical conditions.

He was our blank canvas.

There is a happy ending to my story. I am so proud to be able to say that I am now a father. In February 2021, my wife gave birth to our beautiful twins, a boy and a girl, Ray and

Evelyn. It is a truly amazing feeling, and I love them both so much. I would not change my journey for anything, as it led me on the path to our children and I am exactly where I should be. Everything that happened made me a better person, a better husband and a better father.

I have always known that I am a resilient person. I can bounce back to my baseline after taking a knock. But infertility has shown me that I do not want to just get back to the baseline, I want to grow as a result. I am stronger and I have moved that baseline up a few levels. This will serve me well for any future challenges and it has made me a more open person. I now talk to my wife more freely, sharing my thoughts and concerns. It is no longer about keeping a stiff upper lip because 'that's what men do'. This will translate well into my newfound role as a father and how I raise my twins to become well-rounded, strong characters.

I realise that everything I have gone through has been merely a sequence of events and how I viewed them was a matter of perception. Any event is inanimate. Objective. Binary. It simply is what it is. It is our perceiving eye that makes that event a positive or negative experience, which is usually based on subconscious behaviours learned over time through society, peers and life experiences. I have now chosen to view my experience as a positive one.

I have set up a website www.knackeredknackers.co.uk, sharing my thoughts, to help others that may be going through the same, as well as a regular support group meeting for men. Men experiencing infertility must not suffer in silence. It is not your fault. Have a conversation. That is the first step to understanding and healing. Whether those conversations are with your partner, a friend, a therapist or someone like me.

There are many ways of making a family – each one is as special as the next.

Sarah's Reflections

Setbacks and getbacks. Choices are endless, but sometimes the path you want to take is blocked. How you react to your setbacks can dramatically change the outcome. Tough times are challenging, but that does not mean you have to give up. Being open to possibilities lights up new pathways and then, all of a sudden, things click into place which enable you to get back what you desire the most.

Mind leaps. This does not have to be anything 'Woo, woo!' but mastering your mindset is essential to help you move forward. As Shaun shared, it can be the simple thing of acknowledging and accepting that gives a sense of relief. You can still feel loss but, if you stare into your past, it will haunt you. You cannot change what has happened but, if you can nurture your mind and find new practices, it is a good start to making you think and feel differently.

Consistency crown. Overwhelm when you are feeling vulnerable can be stifling. The trick is to go slowly and be consistent, as a small amount of momentum will keep you going. If you stop, then nothing changes. If you continue, then you give yourself the best chance of success.

Final Reflections

I have learned a lot from writing this book. It has been a labour of love which has changed my outlook on life. Everyone has to deal with difficulty but, for many, the most painful times are the most private. To be given a glimpse into 21 lives is both humbling and inspiring. It creates a powerful mosaic of shared humanity and mutual understanding. Each story showcases the fragile challenges and emotions that bring us together.

I was fascinated to discover strong similarities weaving through the stories. Each contributor described their lowest points and exposed their vulnerability, yet they still wanted to embrace life, search for possibilities, discover meaning and find acceptance to be able to move forward. Strong words such as perspective, courage, self-belief and freedom spring out of the chapters, but there is a fundamental point that each one of them mention. They all had hope!

This is the important realisation and the answer to my question right at the start.

What makes a person determined to get back up?

When you choose hope that makes the difference.

Hope is the driving force and springs you into action.

It gives you an expectation and guides you to believe there is a way.

Inside these pages are valuable insights which hopefully have made you stop and think about your own experiences. Every day you learn, evolve and grow. Dealing with difficulty and trauma stops you in your tracks, but shows you what matters and makes you re-evaluate your life. It can be a real turning point. It is the coping mechanisms in your **Toolbox of Life** that will power you on. It is important you keep filling your toolbox.

I would like you to ponder these questions.

Were there any chapters that stood out?

Is there a person you felt connected to in some way?

Maybe a story that made you think about your own life?

Is there anything you want to focus on and change?

What can you add to your **Toolbox of Life**?

There is a real sense of unity within these pages. Sometimes you must experience darkness to see the light. I hope this book helps you to see the blue skies and sunshine in your life.

Blue skies

Smiling at me

Nothing but blue skies

Do I see

Blue birds

Singing a song

Nothing but blue birds

All day long

Blue days

All of them gone

Nothing but blue skies

From now on

Blue Skies, written by Irving Berlin

Featured in the film *Patch Adams*

Useful Resources

Book recommendations

Adoption Trauma – Fiona Myles

Atomic Habits – James Clear

Energize – Simon Alexander Ong

Feel the Fear and Do It Anyway – Susan Jeffers

Flip It – Michael Heppell

Ikigai – Hector Garcia and Francesc Miralles

Sixteen Days – Dr Victoria Wilson-Crane

S.U.M.O. – Paul McGee

T is for Transformation – Shaun T

The 5 Second Rule – Mel Robbins

The Happy Me Project – Holly Matthews

The Miracle Morning – Hal Elrod

This One Wild and Precious Life – Sarah Wilson

You Only Live Thrice – Karl Perry

Support groups

Action for Happiness www.actionforhappiness.org

Adoption UK www.adoptionuk.org

Cancer Research UK www.cancerresearchuk.org

Cruse www.cruse.org.uk

METUP UK www.metupuk.org.uk

Mind www.mind.org.uk

Multiple Sclerosis Trust www.mstrust.org.uk

Renal Support Network www.rsnhope.org

Samaritans www.samaritans.org

Scottish Action for Mental Health www.samh.org.uk

Survivors of Bereavement by Suicide (SoBS) www.uksobs.org

Acknowledgements

My life is magical because of Edward. I dreamt of having a child and I look at my son's face and feel the deepest happiness, warmth and glow. An outpouring of love, a real sense of belonging and protection. We were meant to find each other. His zest for life and curiosity are a constant source of motivation, spreading joy to everyone he meets.

My hubby Steve. We are ying and yang, but together we make perfect sense. I drive him potty at times, but he would not go anywhere or do anything without my planning. He is patient (our 'in' joke), generous, loving, kind and keeps me from jumping on every idea I come up with. My sounding board for this whole book. He pushed me to keep going.

My mum. I see recognition in her eyes and am pleased to still get a hug and kiss, but sadly dementia has taken her to a faraway place. I miss us being able to chat together, but I know she would have been proud of me as an author. I have fond memories of dancing around the kitchen and calling each other pet names. My mum shaped me into the person I am today. Thank you for showing me lots of love.

Michael Heppell. My mentor. My friend. Who gave me the tools to write my first book and sparked my creativity. Listened and encouraged when I was feeling broken. Made me believe in myself again and have the confidence to follow my dreams. Challenged me to do something incredible with this book and, of course, he was right. He inspires me to be brilliant every day.

Matt Bird (Goose). A genius with typesetting and awesome friend who always has time to listen and help. He was super patient when I needed it the most. I definitely owe him a few rums and extra mince pies.

Christine Beech. An amazing lady who has a great way with finding the right words. I always feel reassured when I know she has cast her eyes on everything I have written.

Des Reynolds. An invaluable supporter. He listened, encouraged, offered great suggestions, helped with the first edit and made me see more clearly.

Jenn Garside. The design queen who has rescued me more than once.

Rob Townsend. My website guru who always has an answer to my random questions.

The Write That Book Alumni. You are superstars.

Hepps Hoodies and Storm Surfers. My online writing companions. We learnt how to write together and now keep each other sane when we lose momentum: Matt Bird, Richard Thomas, Ian Pilbeam, Ildiko SpinFisher, Jeannie Duncanson, Nichola Kingsbury, Maureen Gill, Audrey Macnaughton, Diane Hull, Nick Finney, Sheila Starr, Christine Beech and Gill Westlake.

A big thank you to the 21 amazing contributors who without their willingness to share their lives, this book would not be in existence. You have all made me a better person.

Joshua Robertson, Anna Garratt, Gloria Battini, Karl Perry, Anne Stephens, Paola Palmieri, Emma Morgan, Fiona Myles, Etya Vaserman Krichmar, Richard Thomas, Des Reynolds, Chris Duncan, Tanith Lee, Carly Michael, Marc Skinner, Jan

Ross, Fiona Setch, Indira Mahun, Ray Vincent, Kathleen Findlay and Shaun Greenaway.

A special mention goes to Mary Huckle, who was one of the first people I approached to be a contributor. She wrote the start of her chapter but was unable to continue due to her intense cancer treatment. A strong and determined woman with a beaming smile and big heart; she was an inspiration to me and many others. She raised awareness to empower women and worked closely with METUP UK, who support people with secondary cancer. Sadly, Mary passed away in June 2023. Forever missed, but never forgotten.

Life is nothing short of extraordinary, with valuable lessons. I have realised that every person I meet opens my eyes a bit wider. This book may have taken three years to publish but, in the end, the pace was exactly right as it allowed me to appreciate the joyous journey much more. I hope you have enjoyed the journey too.

Please keep filling up your Toolbox of Life.

About the Author

Sarah McGeough is from Leytonstone, East London, but now lives in East Sussex, with her husband Steve and son Edward. She describes living in Hove as her 'Happy Place'.

'The best days are ones with no plans, a stroll by the sea, maybe dipping our toes in the water.'

Her passion for writing was reignited in May 2020, by joining Michael Heppell's Write That Book Masterclass. This led to the creation of *Eddy Finds a Family* and *Eddy Feels at Home*, which form *The Flamingo Family* children's book series, with more planned in the pipeline.

'Adopting our son has been the most rewarding experience. I created my books to support him through his journey and help families to understand adoption in a fun and engaging way.'

Sarah is a fun-loving super planner, Florida fan who loves new adventures. She wears many hats; with a background in HR, she is a personal performance coach, author, project leader, book coach and creator of *Write Now Coaching* and takes great pride in encouraging fellow writers to release their inner author.

Sarah has been *Knocked Sideways* many times and knows how serious trauma can impact your whole world. It is scary to be in that space where you have no idea what to do next. She felt compelled to write this book, to show that there are ways to recover and find happiness again.

'Being *knocked sideways* made me realise that life is precious time and I have to grab every opportunity.'

The Flamingo Family

Write Now Coaching

Please scan for more information.

You can contact Sarah at sarah@writenowcoaching.co.uk